# YOUR KNOWLEDGE HAS V

- We will publish your bachelor's and master's thesis, essays and papers

- Your own eBook and book - sold worldwide in all relevant shops

- Earn money with each sale

## Upload your text at www.GRIN.com and publish for free

**Bibliographic information published by the German National Library:**

The German National Library lists this publication in the National Bibliography; detailed bibliographic data are available on the Internet at http://dnb.dnb.de .

**Imprint:**

Copyright © 2009 GRIN Verlag, Open Publishing GmbH
Print and binding: Books on Demand GmbH, Norderstedt Germany
ISBN: 9783640477098

Jochen Höfenstock

**An efficient holistic implementation plan of the ITIL®
framework version 3 for SMB**

GRIN Publishing

**GRIN - Your knowledge has value**

Since its foundation in 1998, GRIN has specialized in publishing academic texts by students, college teachers and other academics as e-book and printed book. The website www.grin.com is an ideal platform for presenting term papers, final papers, scientific essays, dissertations and specialist books.

**Visit us on the internet:**

http://www.grin.com/

http://www.facebook.com/grincom

http://www.twitter.com/grin_com

# An efficient holistic implementation plan of the ITIL framework version 3 for small and medium-sized business (SMB) in due consideration of all coherences and dependences to assure optimum quality of implementation

**Diplomarbeit**

Zur Erlangung des akademischen Grades

## Magister/Magistra für wirtschaftswissenschaftliche Berufe (FH)

Eingereicht von: **Jochen Höfenstock**

im Fachbereich: Informationstechnik

am Fachhochschulstudiengang „Projektmanagement und Informationstechnik"

Kennzahl des Fachhochschul-Studienganges: 0119

Erhalter: Fachhochschule des bfi Wien GesmbH

1020 Wien, Wohlmutstrasse 22

August, 26th 2009

*... for Ilse.*

# Abstract

The IT Infrastructure Library (ITIL) framework is a defacto standard for a holistic
Service Management approach. In its third version a five stage lifecycle model
provides principles, roles, processes and functions next to a plurality of information
for the history of a service from the cradle to the grave. Preceding activities ensure
an efficient implementation of ITIL framework for different kinds of management
systems used by IT departments or service providers for small and medium-sized
business (SMB). This master thesis reviews the corresponding theory of ITIL and
organisational change management as well as project management methods
necessary for ITIL framework implementation. Most small and medium-sized
businesses rush into the implementation of ITIL framework because an essential
analytic planning was not or ineffectually done. The dependences and coherences
between the Service Strategy, Service Design, Service Transition, Service Operation
as well as Continual Service Improvement allege how to efficiently implement the
holistic ITIL framework.

Based on a survey of SMBs experiences and level of organisational maturity this
information gets combined and framed in an implementation plan in due
consideration of all coherences and dependencies to assure optimum quality of
implementation. With such a plan, SMBs are in a position to generate as much as
possible achievement compared with an adequate scale of effort. SMB has also the
assurance that only the appropriate parts of ITIL framework are affected for its
System or Service Management approach. The chain of causation starts with a
summary of all five ITIL lifecycle stages and its interfaces next to a survey of SMB's
experiences with such a framework and level of organisational maturity. It ends with
an implementation plan based on the participators statements and adequate project
management methods for definition of objectives, pinpointing of dependencies, object
and work breakdown structures and environment analysis. My major conclusion of
this master thesis is that costs saving characteristics of ITIL framework do not appear
by ITIL framework implementation. They appear in case of consistent application.

# Table of contents

Table of contents

Table of contents

Table of contents

# 1 Introduction

## 1.1 Motivation

Communicating with company internal customers and serve them with services in an appropriate way is a challenge for most of Information Technology (IT) departments. The problem thereby is that the company internal customers think and act in business processes which get supported by functions (departments). On the other hand the IT departments think in technologies and act with their software, applications, servers and other IT related miscellaneous IT and telecommunication components.

Company internal customers request cost transparency, business corresponding functionality and quality which are seriously given in the minority of cases. A solution for this purpose is IT Service Management (ITSM), which is philosophically centred on the company internal customer's perspective of IT supporting its business.

The motivation to write this master thesis is to describe how the Information Technology Infrastructure Library (ITIL) framework in version 3 enables ITSM in small and medium-sized business (SMB).

## 1.2 Problem Description

The ITIL framework is the most known model for ITSM. It describes on a conceptual basis how the provided applications and other IT and telecommunication components as well as the staff productivity can be merged to IT Services. The main intention of ITIL is company internal customer orientation and management of IT Services instead of applications or other IT and telecommunication components.

In addition to the improved quality of IT Services and the superior company internal customer orientation, the expenses of formalism and controlling raise due to the complexity of ITIL. This is one of the most reasons for IT departments of SMB not to deal with the ITIL framework in spite of possible improvement of quality.

It is difficult to find out which methods and recommendations of ITIL should get implemented, which should get partly implemented and which should be ignored. All the content of the ITIL publications by the Office of Government Commerce (OGC) interact together and bring along a lot of coherences and dependences.

## 1.3 Objective

The objective of this master thesis is to circumstantiate an efficient holistic implementation plan of the ITIL framework in version 3 for SMB in due consideration of all coherences and dependences to assure optimum quality of implementation. With such a plan, the SMBs are in a position to generate as much as possible achievement compared with an adequate scale of effort. The SMB has also the assurance that only the appropriate parts of ITIL framework are affected.

This implementation plan bases on the identified experiences of SMB with ITIL, their fulfilment of company internal customer needs and the possibilities to reduce the extensiveness of methods and recommendations in due consideration of all coherences and dependences.

## 1.4 Structure of this master thesis

Explaining and circumstantiating the implementation plan of ITIL for SMB, the essential content is structured as described below.

Chapter 1 introduces in the master thesis. It explains the motivation, the problem description, the objective and the structure.

Chapter 2 and 3 gives an overview of ITSM and the ITIL framework in version 3 as a basis for the implementation plan next to the experiences and needs of SMB.

Chapter 4 describes the experiences of SMB with ITIL, their experiences with company internal customer satisfaction and their needs based on a survey.

Chapter 5 describes how the ITIL framework in version 3 has to be tailored and implemented to match the requirements and conditions in due to all coherences and dependences.

Chapter 6 is my conclusion.

# 2 IT Service Management

The terms ITSM, IT Service and others involved are not owned by an author, an organisation or vendor. There are few definitions which describe more or less the same. It is important to understand at the beginning of this master thesis what ITSM exactly is and to know its context.

At first I define for this master thesis, based on the recommended definitions of authors of essential lecture, the terms and their relations and coherences.

The significant lecture concerning this question is coming from the

- International Organization for Standardization (ISO), from the

- Information Technology Service Management Forum (itSMF) and the

- Office of Government Commerce (OGC) – author of ITIL.

(cf. Van Bon et al 2007, p. 321)

The ISO *"...is the world's largest developer and publisher of international standards. It is also a network of the national standards institute of 159 countries as well as a non-governmental organization that forms a bridge between the public and private sectors. It's central secretariat is in Geneva, Switzerland..."* (ISO 2009)

The itSMF is *"...a global, independent, internationally recognized not-for-profit organization dedicated to support the development of IT Service Management, [...]. It consists of a growing number of national chapters (40+), with itSMF International (itSMFI) as the controlling body."* (Van Bon et al 2008, p. 13)

The OGC is *"...an independent office of HM Treasury, established to help Government deliver best value from its spending. [...] OGC provides policy standards and guidance on best practice in procurement, projects and estate management, and monitors and challenges Departments' performance against these standards, grounded in an evidence base of information and assurance."* (OGC 2009)

## 2.1 Definitions of terms by ISO

The ISO defines the term **Service Management** as *"Management of services to meet the business requirements"* (ISO 2005a, p. 3).

The terms **Managed Service, Service** or **IT Service** are used in the same understanding plenty of times but they are not explained exactly nor defined.

## 2.2 Definition of terms by itSMF

The itSMF defines the term **IT Service Management** as *"Service Management is a set of specialized organizational capabilities for providing value to customers in the form of services"* (Cartlidge et al 2007, p. 6).

The term **Value** is described as *"Value is the core of the service concept. From the customer's perspective, value consists of two core components: utility and warranty. Utility is what the customer receives, and warranty is how it is provided."* (Van Bon et al 2008, p. 19).

The term **Service** is described as *"A means of delivering value to customers by facilitating outcomes the customers want to achieve without the ownership of specific costs or risks. Outcomes are possible from the performance of tasks and they are limited by a number of constraints. Services enhance performance and reduce the pressure of constraints. This increases the chances of the desired outcomes being realized."* (Van Bon et al 2008, p. 19).

## 2.3 Definition of terms by OGC

OGC describes the term **IT Service Management** as *"The implementation and management of Quality IT Services that meet the needs of the business. IT Service Management is performed by IT Service Providers through an appropriate mix of people, Process and Information Technology."* (OGC 2007d, p. 243).

The term **IT Service** is described as *"A Service provided to one or more Customers by an IT Service Provider. An IT Service is based on the use of Information Technology and supports the Customer's business processes. An IT Service is made* *up from a combination of people, Processes and technology and should be defined in a Service Level Agreement."* (OGC 2007d, p. 243).

The term **Business** is described as *"An overall corporate entity or Organization formed of a number of business units. In the context of ITSM, the term business includes public sector and not-for-profit organizations, as well as companies. An IT Service Provider provides IT Services to a Customer within a business. The IT Service Provider may be part of the same business as its Customer (internal Service Provider), or part of another business (external Service Provider)"* (OGC 2007d, p. 235).

The term **Customer** is described as *"Someone who buys goods or Services. The Customer of an IT Service Provider is the person or group that defines and agrees the Service Level Targets. The term Customers is also sometimes informally used to mean Users, for example 'this is a Customer-focused Organization'"* (OGC 2007d, p. 239).

The IT Service continuum differentiates between three management strategies. The IT Systems Management, the IT Service Management and the Business Service Management (see Figure 1). The IT management continuum says that the Value to Business forces up from IT Systems Management to IT Service Management and finally to Business Service Management (cf. OGC 2007d, p. 119ff.).

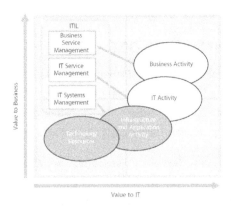

**Figure 1: The IT management continuum (OGC 2007d, p. 123)**

5

Managing all relevant IT components (e.g. servers, applications) and make sure their operational availability, functionality and reliability is given, is understood as **IT Systems Management**. Hereby the focus is on technical environment and not directly on business (cf. OGC 2007d, p. 119ff.).

While managing IT components operational availability, functionality and reliability, the management of IT Services is centred on business needs. It is not enough to focus on operational information about the infrastructure's health even though it is very critical. If there is a link between the activities of an internal IT Service Provider with the objectives of business and all services and IT components are combined in a cohesive set, it concerns the **IT Service Management** (cf. OGC 2007d, p. 119ff.).

**Business Service Management** combines the business process activities and IT Services to a manageable set. While during IT Service Management the customer centric focusing of IT Services is the essential, at business Service Management the focus lies on enabling and management of end-to-end business processes. The Service responsible manages not only IT Services but rather completely business process activities. This is called business services (cf. OGC 2007d, p. 119ff.).

# 3 ITIL framework in version 3

This chapter describes the ITIL framework in version 3. The main publication by OGC counts more than 1600 pages with details on the management system IT Service Management, methods for implementing and executing as well as principles, best practice proposals and recommendations for organisation changes and technology. From this angle it would be impossible to address all information in detail within this chapter. For the conclusion of this master thesis it is important to get an overview about the ITIL theory in its entirety but not in detail. ITIL framework in version 3 is the actual publication of OGC and describes ITSM practices for the IT Service Provider, irrespective of its situation as internal or external provider. ITIL version 1 and version 2 have been developed in the United Kingdom during the late 1980s, the early 1990s and 2002 by the Government Information Technology Infrastructure Management Methodology (GITMM) which is known as OGC nowadays. ITIL in version 3 is advancement, has been published in 2007 and consists of the following publications:

- Introduction to ITIL Service Management Practices

The ITIL Service Management practices core guidance:

- Service Strategy (SS)

- Service Design (SD)

- Service Transition (ST)

- Service Operation (SO)

- Continual Service Improvement (CSI)

(cf. Van Bon et al 2008, p.13ff., OGC 2007f, p. 3ff.)

Having the best technology in place does not ensure a sustainable service for business. It is not just the technology that makes service reliable. It is how they are managed. This is Service Management. The aim of the ITIL practices is the provision of stable and reliable services which were seen as a trusted utility by business.

ITIL mentions best practices applicable to all types of Service Providers. The ITIL Service Management Practices are structured in three main sets:

- ITIL Service Management practices - core guidance are structured in form of a lifecycle. They are the main publications by OGC (Introduction to ITIL Service Management Practices, Service Strategy, Service Design, Service Transition, Service Operation and Continual Service Improvement (see Figure 2)).

- ITIL Service Management practices – complementary guidance are a living library and support and enhance the guidance in the ITIL core for specific industry sectors, organisation types, operating models and technology architectures. This master thesis does not further respond on the complementary guidance.

- ITIL web support services are case studies, templates and a discussion forum for a closed user group on the Internet (www.itil-live-portal.com). The subscription is with costs. This master thesis does not further respond on the complementary guidance.

(cf. OGC 2007f, p. 4ff.)

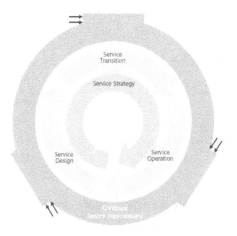

**Figure 2: The Service Lifecycle (OGC 2007d, p. 24)**

8

## 3.1 Service Strategy

Service Strategy (SS) is critical for all ITIL service lifecycle processes. It delivers guidance with designing, developing and implementing Service Management as the centre of the lifecycle. The mission of Service Strategy is to enable an organisation to achieve and maintain a strategic advantage. For that, Service Strategy describes what should be provided to the customers and of what it should consist. Furthermore the kinds of Service Provider types, service provisioning models and organisational improvements are described and recommended (cf. OGC 2007d, p. 1ff.). Service Management has to provide a value to the customer. **Service value** creation is the result of a combination of utility and warranty of an IT Service (see Figure 3). The Value creation depends on either of both, they are necessary, neither is sufficient by itself. Utility as well as warranty have to be considered as a separate factor of value.

- Utility is the characteristic of an IT Service which have a positive effect on business. The removal or partly removal of constraints on service performance is also appreciated as a positive effect. The causal effect of utility is the increase of a possible profit.

- Warranty means IT Services are available with adequate capacity in continuity and security when needed. The causal effect of warranty is the decline in possible losses.

(cf. OGC 2007d, p. 17, Van Bon et al 2008, p. 24ff.)

**Figure 3: Logic of value creation through services (OGC 2007d, p.17)**

ITIL recommends to cognize the **value network** to enable relationships with customers, suppliers and organisation internal. The value creation is done by exchange of knowledge, information and goods or services between partners/suppliers, customers and groups or organisations (cf. OGC 2007d, p. 47ff.).

**Service assets** are used by the Service Provider to create the utility and warranty for value creation: resources and capabilities.

- Resources are the components which produce the IT Service. These components are management, organisational structures, processes and knowledge.

- Capabilities are the capacities of a Service Provider to enable the resources to generate the value for business at an adequate level of quality (availability, capacity, continuity, security). These are financial capital, infrastructure, applications and information.

(cf. OGC 2007d, p. 38ff.)

ITIL distinguishes between three types of Service Providers which provide these service assets to customers. This is done to understand which aspects of Service Management are reasonably applicable to organisations and business of a Service Provider. This separation is done to facilitate customers for their decision on Service Providers – matching need to capability (see Figure 4).

- Type I – internal Service Providers are providers who deliver the IT Services within their own business units.

- Type II – shared services units are providers who deliver their IT Services to more than one business unit.

- Type III – external Service Providers are providers who deliver their IT Services to external customers in competing business

(cf. OGC 2007d, p. 41ff.)

| From/To | Type I | Type II | Type III |
|---|---|---|---|
| Type I | Functional reorganization | Disaggregation | Outsourcing |
| Type II | Aggregation | Corporate reorganization | Outsourcing |
| Type III | Insourcing | Insourcing | Value net reconfiguration |

**Figure 4: Customer decisions on Service Provider types (OGC 2007d, p. 45)**

Customers should select by the **model of service provisioning**, which IT Services should be sourced and delivered. Service Providers use these models under consideration of financial management impacts of on-shore, off-shore or near shore variants.

- Managed Services; Provision of an IT Service to a business unit which requires it for itself. Funding is also done by the business unit.

- Shared Services; Provision of multiple IT Services to one or more business units. Funding of the IT Services is done subdivided by specific agreements.

- Utility based provisioning; Provision of IT Services to one or more business units on the basis of how much is required. Funding of the IT Service is done by utilisation.

(cf. OGC 2007d, p. 104ff.)

To ensure high quality of realised activities, ITIL recommends based on lifecycle phase processes being carried out that all issues concerning the topics are fulfilled. For SS these processes are Financial Management, Return on Investment (ROI), Demand Management and Service Portfolio Management (SPM).

## 3.1.1 Financial Management

Financial Management does not exist solely within the holistic financial domain. For an internal Service Provider the IT-Financial Management is an integrated part of company's financial management. It covers all activities which are responsible for managing a provider's budget, charging and accounting requirements.

IT provides operational forecasting, the value of IT Services as well as the value of the underlying assets in form of financial terms to the customer and provider. It provides also information regarding efficient and cost-effective service delivery and allocates expenditures directly to IT Services. The basic concepts are:

- Provisioning values are the creation costs of an IT Service (e.g. hardware costs, software licence costs, annual maintenance costs, personnel costs, facility costs, tax funds, compliance costs)

- Service value potential is the added value for the customer based on its perception of value from the IT Service or expected utility and warranty of usage of the IT Service, compared with the customer's assets.

(cf. OGC 2007d, p. 97ff.)

All costing and budgeting activities which are typically for an Service Provider bases on the IT Services. So, a correct funding for the delivery of an IT Service calls for analysis and searching for the many variables that have an impact on the IT Service costs. **Variable Cost Dynamics (VCD)** do so by taking an insight on direct respectively indirect costs, labor costs, variable costs as well as on the complexity of delivery and utilisation (cf. OGC 2007d, p. 103ff.).

## 3.1.2 Return on Investment

*"ROI is used as a measure of the ability to use assets to generate additional value. In the simplest sense, it is the net profit of an investment divided by the net worth of the assets invested. The resulting percentage is applied to either additional top-line revenue or the elimination of bottom-line cost.*

- *Business case – a means to identify business imperatives that depend on Service Management*

- *Pre-Programme ROI – techniques for quantitatively analysing an investment in Service Management*

- *Post-Programme ROI – techniques for retroactively analysing an investment in Service Management."*

(OGC 2007d, p. 112)

### 3.1.3 Demand Management

It is not possible to create IT Services and store them until customers demand evolves. Within IT the production and consumption of IT Services is done synchronously and dealing with demands has to be done in a pull-system, in which consumption cycles initiate production cycles (see Figure 5). Demand Management has to understand customer's demands and has an impact on them. This is done by analysis of customer's business and user profiles as well as by setting different charging models to encourage customers to use IT Services at less busy times. The basic concepts are:

- Service packages consist of a Service Level Package and one or more core and supporting IT Services. It is a detailed description of an IT Service provided for customers.

- Service Level Packages (SLP) are designed to be up to the business activity's mark and describe a defined level of utility and warranty for a particular service package.

- Core service Package (CSP) is a detailed description of a core service that is shared by Service Level Packages.

- Line of Service (LOS) is a set of different entities of a core or supporting service that supports different Service Packages.

(cf. OGC 2007d, p. 129ff.)

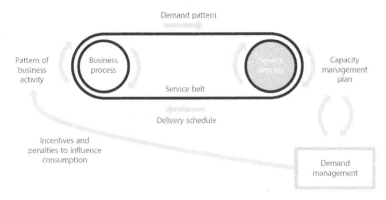

**Figure 5: Business activity influences patterns of demand for services**
**(OGC 2007d, p. 130)**

## 3.1.4 Service Portfolio Management

The aim of Service Portfolio Management is the creation of maximum value by managing risks and costs. It shows IT Services in term of business value. Service Portfolio Management is an ongoing process for investments across the lifecycle of an IT Service. It guides the IT Service from concept via design, transition and operational status till its retirement. Service Portfolio Management directs in terms of financial values (cf. OGC 2007d, p. 119ff.). The main utilities (see Figure 6) are:

- Service Catalogue is a detailed overview of all actual provided IT Services of a Service Provider and is visible to the customer.

- Service Pipeline consists of all IT Services that are in planning or development. It is a strategic foresight, all IT Services within the pipeline get applied into the production via the Service Transition lifecycle phase.

- Retired Services are phased out and were not offered to the customer. It is necessary to guarantee all agreements with customers to control phased out IT Services within the Service Transition lifecycle phase.

(cf. OGC 2007d, p. 119ff.)

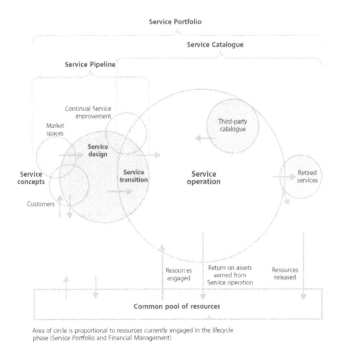

**Figure 6: Service pipeline and service catalogue (OGC 2007d, p. 74)**

## 3.2 Service Design

Service Design (SD) is next to SS a stage in the Service lifecycle and supports business change process as an important facilitator (see Figure 7). Within this lifecycle stage, appropriate and innovative IT Services including their architectures, processes, policies and documentations are designed according actual and upcoming requirements by business.

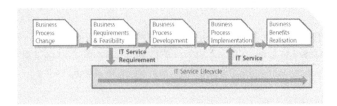

**Figure 7: The business change process (OGC 2007b, p. 23)**

This stage starts with a set of business requirements and ends with the designed service solution in form of a Service Design Package (SDP) ready to handover to the next stage, Service Transition (see chapter 3.3) (cf. OGC 2007b, p. 11ff.). A Service Design Package is *"Document(s) defining all aspects of an IT Service and its Requirements through each stage of its Lifecycle. A Service Design Package is produced for each new IT Service, major Change, or IT Service Retirement."* (OGC 2007b, p. 309).

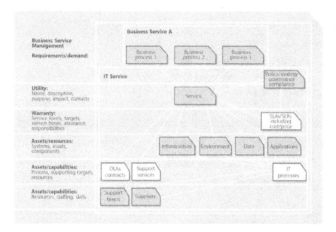

**Figure 8: Service Composition (OGC 2007b, p. 24)**

As described in chapter 3.1, an IT Service provides a required utility under respect of an agreed warranty, produced by capabilities with the resources (see Figure 8). How to develop such an IT Service depends strongly on the decision which service delivery model is chosen. ITIL characterises the following main service delivery strategies:

- Insourcing; Internal resources are used for design, transition, operation and improvement for IT Service.

- Outsourcing; The opposite of insourcing is outsourcing. Thus, design, transition and operation for the IT Service is done by external organisations.

- Co-sourcing; A combination of insourcing and outsourcing in which various outsourcing organisations work together through the whole lifecycle.

- Partnership or multi sourcing; Multiple organisations make formal agreements with focus on strategic partnerships (to create new market opportunities).

- Business Process Outsourcing (BPO); An external organisation takes over a business process or a part of it in order to save costs partly (eg. call center).

- Application Service Provision (ASP); IT-based IT Services are offered to customers over a technical network.

- Knowledge Process Outsourcing (KPO); Is an enhancement of Business Process Outsourcing and offers knowledge of a (part of a) process or knowledge of an entire work area.

(cf. OGC 2007b, p. 50ff.)

The Service Design lifecycle stage follows the demand management of Service Strategy and proceeds to Service Transition stage. Trough the Service Design stage the Design Package of Demand Management will be aligned to the Service Portfolio and designed and developed with the aid of the following processes (see Figure 9):

- Service Catalogue Management (SCM)

- Service Level Management (SLM)

- Capacity Management

- Availability Management

- IT Service Continuity Management

- Information Security Management

- Supplier Management

(cf. OGC 2007b, p. 59ff.)

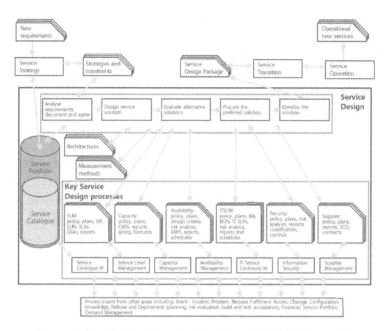

**Figure 9: Service Design - the big picture (OGC 2007b, p. 60)**

## 3.2.1 Service Catalogue Management

The Service Catalogue Management (SCM) within Service Design provides a single, consistent source of information on all active IT Services and ensures that it is available for whom it concerns. The Service Catalogue is a subset of the Service Portfolio and consists of active IT Services. The Service Portfolio (as described in chapter 3.1.4) describes the entire process, starting with business requirements and execution of IT Services. It contains all active and inactive (in pipeline, retired) IT Services in their various phases. SCM includes the following activities:

(1) Definition of an IT Service including all interfaces and dependencies between the IT Services and the underlying core and supporting services.

(2) Maintenance of the Service Catalogue.

(3) Maintenance of the dependencies and consistency between the catalogue and the Service Portfolio.

The Service Catalogue has two aspects (see Figure 10):

- The Business Service Catalogue; Contains details of all IT Services (also named as Business Services in some parts of the ITIL publications) which are actually provided to business with relationships to business units and business processes. The Business Service Catalogue can also be seen as the customer's view to the Service Catalogue.

- The Technical Service Catalogue; Contains all components which are necessary to enable an IT Service. These components are the core services and the supporting services. Core services deliver the basic outcomes desired by the customers for which they are willing to pay. Supporting services either enable or enhance value proposition. Core and/or supporting services are the capabilities and resources of an IT Service (see Figure 8).

(cf. OGC 2007b, p. 59ff.)

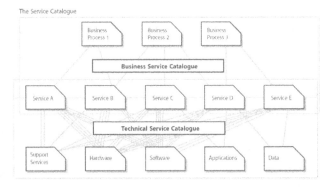

**Figure 10: The Business Service Catalogue and the Technical Service Catalogue (OGC 2007b, p. 62)**

## 3.2.2 Service Level Management

Service Level Management (SLM) ensures that an agreed service level is written, reviewed and reported at regular intervals. Within the scope of Service Level management are external interfaces of a Service Provider to customers and suppliers as well as internal interfaces to another parts of its organisation.

The distinction is done by:

- Service Level Agreements (SLA); Agreements which cover the utility and warranty between the customer and the Service Provider.

- Operational Level Agreements (OLA); Agreements which define the goods or services that are provided from a department to another within the same organisation.

- Underpinning Contracts (UC); Agreements which manage the delivery or support of supplier's benefits.

The OLA and UC define targets and responsibilities that are required to meet agreed service level targets in an SLA. (cf. OGC 2007b, p. 65ff.). The methods, activities and techniques within SLM are:

(1) Design of SLA frameworks; Design of an appropriate SLA structure to cover all services and customers in a manner best suited to organisational needs:

  a. Service-based SLAs; One SLA covers one IT Service for all customers of that IT Service.

  b. Customer-based SLAs; One SLA with one customer containing all IT Services it uses.

  c. Multi-level SLAs; Three layer structure: **Corporate layer** covers all SLM issues appropriate to every customer. **Customer layer** covers all SLM issues appropriate to particular customer groups, business units or domains. **Service layer** covers all SLM issues to a specific IT Service in relation to a defined entity or the customer layer.

(2) Determining, documenting and agreeing requirements for new services and production of Service Level Requirements (SLR); After completion of the service catalogue and SLA frameworks, the SLRs have to be discussed and agreed with the customer. These SLRs are the basis for the next steps.

(3) Monitoring service performance against SLA and reporting; Measurement of all Service Level Requirements and deviations from thresholds.

(4) Reviewing of the underlying agreements; Regular check if the IT Service underlying agreements (OLA, UC) are within constraints deduced from the accordant SLA.

(5) Reviewing and improving IT Services; Consulting the customer to evaluate the utility and warranty of the IT Service on a regular basis. Measures derived from these reviews have to be documented and managed in a Service Improvement Plan (SIP).

(cf. OGC 2007b, p. 66ff.)

## 3.2.3 Capacity Management

During the Service Design stage, Capacity Management plans the business, service and component capacities deduced from the Service Packages (see chapter 3.1.3). Capacity Management is then executed across the whole lifecycle. The most important element within the Capacity Management is the Capacity Management Information System (CMIS) that provides relevant and aligned information for the management of Business, service and component capacities. Therefore the three sub processes are:

- Business Capacity Management; With a focus on current and future business needs, the customer requirements are translated into specifications for IT Services.

- Service Capacity Management; Based on the specifications from BCM, Service Capacity Management monitors IT Services, measures their performance, analyse and reports them. This is done to ensure that the IT Services meet their SLA targets

- Component Capacity Management; CCM does basically the same as SCM but with focus on components that enables IT Services such as processors, networks, and bandwidth.

So the main activities within the Capacity Management are:

(1) reactive actions, such as monitoring and measuring

(2) proactive activities, such as predicting future requirements and trends

(cf. OGC 2007b, p. 79ff.)

### 3.2.4 Availability Management

While Capacity Management deals with current and future business needs on capacity issues, Availability Management proceeds with needs on availability. This process has to ensure that the agreed level of IT Service availability meets its agreed targets across the entire lifecycle. Availability Management includes designing, implementing, measuring, managing and improving IT Services and its components availability as an important part of the SDP. Therefore the following aspects get monitored, measured, analysed and reported:

- Availability; The ability of the IT Service and its components to be available when required.

- Reliability; The time period while an IT Service and its components are available without interruption (mean time between system incidents (MTBSI) and mean time between failures (MTBF)).

- Maintainability; How effectively and quickly an IT Service and its components can be restored after a failure (Mean time to restore service (MTRS)).

- Serviceability; The ability of an external IT Service Provider or supplier to meet the terms of their UCs.

To optimise the availability of IT Services, a detailed analysis of an incident lifecycle is required. The standardised way to spread an incident is described in the expanded incident lifecycle which defines the start and end of up and down time as well as the different steps within. The unavailability of an IT Service can be reduced by detecting root causes for high unavailability (see Figure 11) (cf. OGC 2007b, p. 100f.).

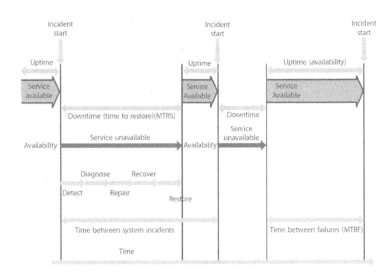

**Figure 11: The expanded incident lifecycle (OGC 2007b, p. 106)**

For analysing an incident and improving of the aspects listed above, ITIL recommends the following metrics:

$$\text{Availability (\%)} = \frac{\text{Agreed Service Time (AST)} - \text{downtime}}{\text{Agreed Service Time (AST)}} \times 100$$

$$\text{MTBSI (hours)} = \frac{\text{Available time in hours}}{\text{number of breaks}}$$

$$\text{MTBF (hours)} = \frac{\text{Available time in hours} - \text{total downtime in hours}}{\text{number of breaks}}$$

$$\text{MTRS (hours)} = \frac{\text{Total downtime in hours}}{\text{number of breaks}}$$

(cf. OGC 2007b, p. 100f.)

All these aspects and metrics are aligned and stored in the Availability Management Information System (AMIS). Therefore the main activities are:

- Reactive activities such as monitoring, measuring, analysing and reporting the availability of IT Service, analysing unavailability and Service Failure Analysis (SFA).

- Proactive activities such as designing for availability, Component Failure Impact Analysis (CFIA), Single Point of Failure (SPOF) analysis, Fault Tree Analysis (FTA), risk analysis and management, production of the Projected Service Availability (PSA) document and continuous reviewing and improvement.

(cf. OGC 2007b, p. 97ff.)

### 3.2.5 IT Service Continuity Management

IT Service Continuity Management (ITSCM) ensures and maintains an appropriate recovery capability within IT Services to meet the requirements and timeframes of business in case of a calamity. As the main process interface of the Service Provider it supports the overall business continuity management process of customers. The basic concept is that IT Service continuity and recovery plans have been created and kept continuously aligned with the identified business continuity plans and business priorities. The main activities are:

(1) Initiation; Through this phase the entire organisation defines the policy, specifies conditions and scope, allocates necessary resources and defines an adequate management structure for implementing ITSCM.

(2) Requirements and strategies; Through this phase the business requirements for ITSCM and strategies get determined. ITIL recommends for identification of business requirements a Business Impact Analysis (BIA) and risk estimation. Suitable strategies have to cover risk-reducing measures as well as IT recovery options.

(3) Implementation; Through the implementation phase the ITSCM plan gets created corresponding to the approved strategy. This plan describes disaster organisation as well as which IT Services have to be recommissioned in case of a disaster. If calamities occur, leadership and decision-making processes change. A senior manager has to be in charge for the accomplishment.

(4) Ongoing Operations; To assure an adequate ITSCM plan, education and awareness trainings, regular scenario and walkthrough tests have to be carried out.

(cf. OGC 2007b, p. 125ff.)

## 3.2.6 Information Security Management

The aim of information security management is to keep information security aligned with business security and to ensure that information security is managed effectively. The essential components therefore are:

- An information security policy

- An Information Security Management System (ISMS)

- A comprehensive security strategy

- An effective security organisation

- A set of security controls according to security policy

- A risk management

- Training and awareness plans

Information security management gets initialised through the service design and has to be done while all follow-up stages of the IT Service lifecycle. For this reason, the ISMS has to be considered during the design of each service, changes of organisation and processes and all other activities which have impact on it. Information security management is not only a technical issue.

The main activities are:

(1) Operation, maintenance and distribution of information security policy

(2) Assessment of information

(3) Implementation and documentation of the security controls in processes, systems, facilities etc.

(4) Monitoring and management of breaches and security incidents

(cf. OGC 2007b, p. 141ff.)

### 3.2.7 Supplier Management

To ensure a seamless quality of IT Services, Service Providers have to pay attention on all involved parties while design, transition and operation stages of the IT Service. These are inter alia suppliers and the services supplied by them have also to be managed. Under consideration of the expectation value network (see chapter 3.1) this should be realised in form of a partnership.

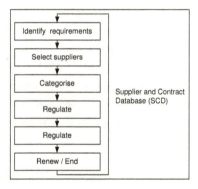

**Figure 12: Contract Lifecycle (own illustration 2009, cf. Van Bon et al 2008, p. 101)**

The basic concept of supplier management is that all activities within have to result from a supplier strategy. To ensure that, important information has to be available for all these activities. A Supplier and Contract Database (SCD) has to be used by each activity within this process (see Figure 12). The essential aim of SLM is drawing up a formal UC which is not covered by supplier management. But it is necessary to identify the performance of suppliers from SLM reviews and bear it in mind during categorisation activities. The categorisation has to point out the impact of a supplier and its services on the Service Provider. Therefore it is necessary to structure all suppliers according to the following focal points:

- Intensity of risks and impact of supplier

- Intensity of value potential and importance of supplier

- Dependency of the supplier from the Service Provider and vice versa

(cf. OGC 2007b, p. 149ff.)

## 3.3  Service Transition

As illustrated in Figure 2, Service Transition is a stage in the lifecycle of an IT Service. The aim of Service Transition is to deliver IT Services which are given over by Service Design in form of an SDP into operational use. It is always important to recognise changed business circumstances, assumptions or requirements during the Service Transition stage because it is the last facility to change required services. ITIL defines the scope of Service Transition as *"Service Transition includes the management and coordination of the processes, systems and functions required for the packaging, building, testing, deployment of a release into production and establish the service specified in the customer and stake-holder requirements."* (Van Bon et al 2007, p. 93) Key Principles of Service Transition are:

- For an effective Service Transition it is essential to know its nature and purpose in terms of the outcomes or removed business constraints and assurances that utilities will be delivered → Understanding all services, their utility and warranty.

- Consistency and comprehensiveness ensure that no services, stake-holders, occurrences are missed out and so cause service failures → Establishment of a formal policy and framework for change implementation.

- Involving all relevant parties, ensuring knowledge availability and reusable work delivers effective Service Transition → Support of knowledge transfer, decision support and reuse of processes and systems.

- Full documentation of proactive determination of likely course corrections → Anticipation and management of course corrections.

- Ensuring involvement of Service Transition through the whole IT Service lifecycle.

(cf. OGC 2007e, p. 24ff., Cartlidge 2007, p.24f.)

The Service Transition stage provides processes which have impact across all lifecycle stages and processes which are mainly focused on its stage. The whole lifecycle processes are:

- Change Management

- Service Asset and Configuration Management (SACM)

- Knowledge Management

Processes focused on Service Transition, but not exclusive to the stage are:

- Transition Planning and Support

- Release and Deployment Management

- Service Validation and Testing

- Evaluation

### 3.3.1 Transition Planning and Support

The transition planning and support process has to ensure that the planning and coordination of resources is done for realisation of all specifications described in the SDP. Additionally the identification, management and minimisation of risks is handled by this process to identify and minimise the risks which can interrupt the service during transition. Within the scope of Service Transition are design specifications as well as management of plans, supporting activities, transition progress, risks, deviations and processes and their supporting systems and tools. Within transition planning and support release (see chapter 3.3.4) guidelines and policies are defined, which should contain at least

- Naming conventions, distinguishing release types (major, minor or emergency release),

- Roles and responsibilities,

- Release cycle,

- Approach for accepting and grouping changes into a release,

- Entry and exit criteria and authority for acceptance of the release into the controlled test, training, disaster recovery and production environment and

- Criteria authorisation for leaving Early Life Support (ELS) and handover to service operation.

Main activities of Service Transition are:

(1) Setup of a transition strategy; The transition strategy defines the global approach to Service Transition and the assignment of resources.

(2) Preparation of Service Transition; The preparation consists of analysis and acceptance of input from other service lifecycle stages; identifying, filing and planning Request for Changes (RfC), monitoring the baseline and transition readiness.

(3) Planning and Coordination of Service Transition; An individual Service Transition plan describes the tasks and activities required to roll out a release in a test and production environment.

(4) Support; Service Transition advises and supports all stake-holders. The planning and support team will provide insight for stake-holders regarding Service Transition processes and supporting systems and tools.

(cf. OGC 2007e, p. 35ff.)

## 3.3.2 Change Management

Change Management enables changes to be made with minimal disruption to IT Services. This process ensures that changes are deployed in a controlled way such as recording, evaluating, authorising, prioritising, planning, testing, implementation and documentation. Therefore it is necessary to have standardised methods for efficient and prompt handling of all changes. Typically the process should be used for defined Configuration Items (CIs) (see chapter 3.3.3). The process addresses all IT Service changes. ITIL defines a Service Change as *"The addition, modification or removal of authorized, planned or supported service or service component and its associated documentation."* (OGC 2007e, p. 43) The ITIL Change Management process scope covers IT Services within the Service Portfolio and Service Operation (see Figure 13). Other changes should be defined by the service provider and managed by appropriate procedures in a narrow reconciliation with the change management process.

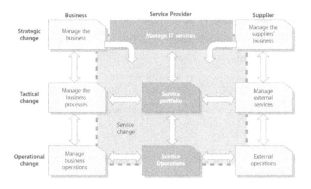

**Figure 13: Scope of change and release management for services**
**(OGC 2007e, p. 43)**

How Service Changes, Changes and CIs are arranged among each other is described in chapter 3.3.3. The basic types of changes are:

- A **Request for Change (RfC)** which is a formal request to change one or more CIs.

- A **normal change** which is the addition, modification, or elimination of an authorised, planned or supporting service (or component) and its related documentation.

- A **standard change** which is a pre-authorised (or pre-approved), low risk and relatively common change. Standardised procedures or work instructions should be in place for it (eg. provision of standard equipment, new user account, password reset).

- An **emergency change** which is a change that must be transferred as soon as possible to resolve a major incident (see chapter 3.4.2) or implement a security patch.

(cf. OGC 2007e, p. 46ff.)

The ITIL approach to manage changes in such a way is shown in Figure 14. Additionally to this proposal, ITIL also defines overall change management activities such as planning and controlling all changes, scheduling of change implementation and releases, measurement and control etc. The typical activities within the change management process are:

(1) Create and record RfC; An individual or department may submit an RfC. All RfCs are registered, prioritised and identifiable. Prioritisation bases on impact and urgency.

(2) Review RfC and change proposal; After registration, stake-holders verify the RfC in respect of illogicality, unfeasibility, unnecessarily or incompleteness.

(3) Assess and evaluate changes; Based on the impact and a risk assessment the change authority determines the change implementation. Potential benefits and costs of the change also have to be included in decision making.

(4) Authorises the change; Formal authorisation of the change. This can be done by a Change Advisory Board (CAB) which is a consultative board that regularly meets to support the change manager. CABs should be in place for all types of changes, especially the Emergency Change Advisory Board (ECAB).

(5) Coordination of change implementation; Handover of approved changes to the relevant responsible for build, test, creation of releases and deployment. All the changes get controlled and managed with the Change Schedule which is a central list of all approved changes and their implementation dates.

(6) Review and closing of implemented change; If a change is successful implemented it can be closed. A post-implementation review (PIR) ascertains that.

(cf. OGC 2007e, p. 48ff.)

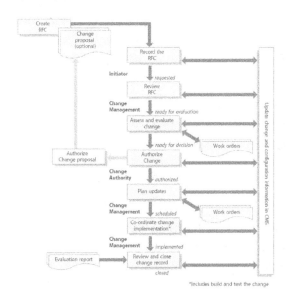

**Figure 14: Example process flow for a normal change (OGC 2007e, p. 49)**

### 3.3.3 Service Asset and Configuration Management

IT is essential within Service Management to administer services which are a combination of people, processes and technology (see chapter 2.3). In case that a part of this combination fails, it is important to get the information as soon as possible which IT Service is affected. In almost the same manner the context of an IT Service is very important during design, operation and especially the transition stage. Therefore a centralised management of all information and components of an IT Service with their relations is required. This is done by the Service Asset and Configuration Management (SACM). The purpose of SACM is to identify and manage service assets and CIs, protecting and ensuring their integrity across the service lifecycle (cf. OGC 2007e, p. 65). The basic concepts of SACM are:

- Configuration Item (CI); A Configuration Item is a service component, asset or other item that is controlled by configuration management. CIs have to be classified to effortless manage and trace them through their lifecycle (e.g. service, hardware, software, documentation, personnel).

- Attribute; An attribute is a piece of information of an CI (e.g. version number, location, build number).

- Relationship; A relationship is a link between two CIs. It describes a dependency between them and shows how CIs work together in the context of an IT Service.

- Configuration Structure; A configuration structure shows all CIs and their relations and hierarchies which build a configuration.

- Configuration baseline; The configuration baseline is the configuration of an IT Service that has been reviewed and agreed. It will be used thereafter as a basis for further activities like restoring an IT Service if a change or release fails.

- Secure libraries and secure stores; Access to items within a secure library or store is restricted. The secure libraries are a collection of software, electronic or document CIs. A secure store locates assets like personal computers or spare parts. They play an important role in security and IT Service continuity management (See chapter 3.2).

- Definitive Media Library (DML); The DML is a secure library that contains all the definitively authorised versions of all media CIs.

- Definitive spares; Definitive spares are spare parts that are identically maintained as their comparatives within the production environment.

- Configuration Management Database (CMDB); A database used to store records of CIs along their lifecycle. One or more CMDBs are part of a Configuration Management System

- Configuration Management System (CMS); A system to manage the whole configuration data as described by a service provider. The CMS also includes information from other processes like Incident, Problem, Change or Release and Deployment Management (see Figure 15).

(cf. OGC 2007e, p. 66ff.)

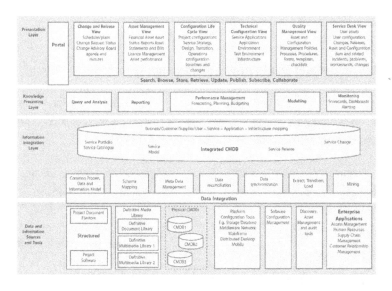

**Figure 15: Example of a Configuration Management System (OGC 2007e, p. 68)**

High-level activities of SACM are:

(1) Management and planning; Making the decision of what level of configuration management is needed and how it will be achieved.

(2) Configuration identification; Determining the configuration structures and selection of CIs, naming conventions, relevant attributes etc.

(3) Configuration control; The activity which setups everything within SACM. It ensures that control mechanisms are in place for adding, adapting or removing CIs with match with the physical world. This activity is triggered by the SACM process for audit as well as the release management.

(4) Status accounting and reporting; The different stages that a CI goes through its lifecycle must be tracked and documented.

(5) Verification and audit; SACM carries out audits for reviewing the consistency between the documented baseline and the physical situation as well as checking that release and configuration documentation is available before rollout of the release.

(cf. OGC 2007e, p. 71ff.)

### 3.3.4 Release and Deployment Management

Through the Release and Deployment process, the capability to provide the required IT Service will be built, tested and delivered. Especially a form of a capability is a release (cf. OGC 2007e, p. 84). The basic concepts are:

- Release; *"A release is a set of new or changed CIs that are tested and will be implemented into production together."* (Van Bon et al 2007, p. 252)

- Release unit; A release unit is part of an IT Service which is included in the release (e.g. for a business critical application it may make sense to include the complete application in the release unit. For a website it may only have to be a single HTML page that is changed)

- Release design; Within release design, the most occurring options for the rollout of releases become sophisticated. ITIL describes the big bang, phased, push and pull as well as automation or manual.

- Release package; A release package is a single release unit or a set of release units. All IT Service components must be taken into account.

- V-model; The V-model (see Figure 16) is an appropriate tool for mapping out the different configuration levels at which buildings and testing must take place. On the left side it starts with specifications and ends with a detailed service design. On the right side it begins with the test activities and finishes with the validation of the left-handed side requirements.

(cf. OGC 2007e, p. 85ff.)

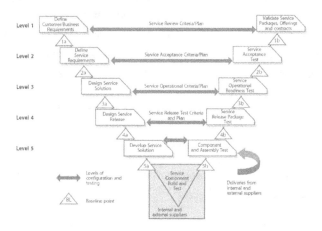

**Figure 16: Service V-model to represent configuration levels and testing (OGC 2007e, p. 92)**

The main process activities are

(1) Planning,

(2) Preparation for building (compilation, testing and deployment),

(3) Building and testing,

(4) Service Testing and pilots,

(5) Planning and preparing the development,

(6) Transfer, deployment and retirement,

(7) Verify deployment,

(8) Early life support and

(9) Review and close.

## 3.3.5 Service Validation and Testing

The key purpose of service validation and testing is to provide objective evidence that the IT Service supports the business requirements including the agreed SLAs. The IT Service is tested against the utilities and warranties set out in the SDP, including business functionality, availability, security, continuity, usability and regression testing. Testing ensures that the IT Services are fit for purpose (utility) and fit for use (warranty) as described in chapter 3.1. Main concepts are:

- Service model; The service model consists of core and supporting services. If a new or changed IT Service is built, this service model is tested in relation to design specifications and requirements.

- Test strategy; The test strategy defines the entire testing approach and the allocation of required resources.

- Test model; The test model consists of a test plan of what has to be tested and test scripts which indicate the method by which each component must be tested. The test model must be structured in a way to ensure that it is reusable for this process. Using the Service V-model (see Figure 16) as the test model, service testing becomes part of the service lifecycle early in the process.

- Service Design Package (See chapter 3.2)

(cf. OGC 2007e, p. 115ff.)

The main activities of service validation and testing are shown in Figure 17 and have not been performed necessarily in this order. They might also take place in parallel to each other.

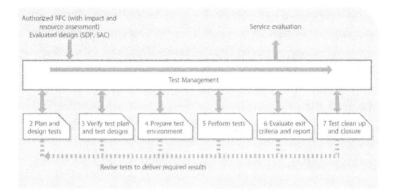

**Figure 17: Example of a validation and testing process (OGC 2007e, p. 133)**

### 3.3.6 Evaluation

Evaluation is a generic process that is intended to verify whether the performance of a service change is acceptable. For example: a proper price/quality-ratio, is the service change continued, is it in use, is it paid for and so on. This process delivers important input for CSI (see chapter 3.5) and continuous improvement of service development and change management process (cf. OGC 2007e, p. 138ff.). The basic concept of Evaluation process is the **Evaluation report** which contains a risk profile, a deviations report, a qualification and validation statement and a recommendation (acceptance or refusal). The Evaluation process mainly consists of the following activities:

(1) Planning the Evaluation; By this activity the intended and unintended effects of a change get analysed. Intended effects must meet the acceptance criteria, unintended effects could be invisible for a time and are difficult to anticipate.

(2) Evaluating the predict performance; Performance of a risk assessment based on the customer's requirements and acceptance criteria. This assessment

report is sent to the change management in case of recognised unacceptable risks to the change or deviations from the acceptance criteria.

(3) Evaluating the actual performance; Service Operation (see chapter 3.4) reports the actual performance of implemented changes. Within this activity the same steps have to be done as before. This step is intended not only to carry out Evaluation before implementation and use the information from daily operations.

(cf. OGC 2007e, p. 139ff.)

### 3.3.7 Knowledge Management

Knowledge Management improves the quality of the decision-making progress by ensuring that the right information is for whom it concerns available during all lifecycle stages. This should be done by sharing experience, knowledge and known errors and workarounds via service knowledge management systems (SKMS) as figured out exemplary in Figure 18.

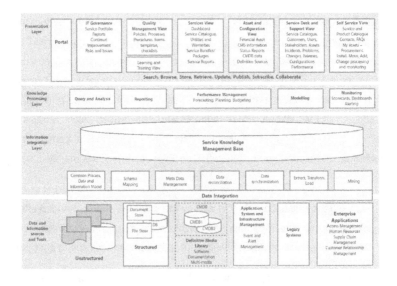

**Figure 18: Service knowledge management system (OGC 2007e, p. 151)**

Knowledge management is visualised by ITIL by using the data-information-knowledge-wisdom-structure (DIKW-structure). Data from metrics are transformed into information (quantity → quality). Knowledge originates by combining information with experience, context, interpretation and reflection. At the time when the right decisions based on the knowledge were made, the level of wisdom is achieved (see Figure 19) (cf. OGC 2007e, p. 145ff.).

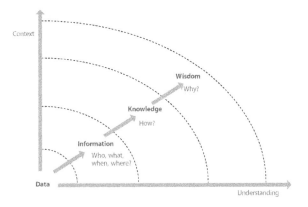

**Figure 19: The flow from data to wisdom (OGC 2007e, p. 147)**

Main activities within knowledge management are:

(1) Knowledge management strategy; Detecting if there is already an overall knowledge strategy in place. If such a strategy is in place, the Service Management knowledge strategy can link into it. The strategy focuses on identification and documentation of relevant knowledge and on the data and information that support this knowledge.

(2) Knowledge transfer; Doing a knowledge gap analysis between sender and receiver and formulate a communication plan to facilitate the knowledge transfer.

(3) Information management; Establishing data and information requirements, defining the information architecture, establishing data and information management procedures, Evaluation and improvement

(4) Use of the SKMS; Providing the SKMS to all relevant lifecycle stages and their processes and activities at the right time for the right recipient. Additionally the training and knowledge material has to be revised regularly.

(cf. OGC 2007e, p. 148ff.)

## 3.4  Service Operation

After handover of the implemented or changed IT Service from Service Transition, Service Operation is providing all concepts, methods and principles to manage and operate them in a day-to-day-operation. But that is not everything: As one stage of the service lifecycle it is responsible for optimisation of costs and quality of IT Services during its operation state. It is important for Service Operation to balance following conflicting goals:

- Internal IT view versus external business view

- Stability versus responsiveness

- Quality of service versus cost of service

- Reactive versus proactive activities

Service Operation as defined by ITIL provides not only applications, technology or infrastructure. Staff members of Service Operations must be aware that they are providing IT Services to the business with the objective to achieve the agreed service level and deliver value to the business (see chapter 3.1) (cf. OGC 2007c, p. 19ff.). Unlike as the other ITIL Service Management practices core guidance (see chapter 3), Service Operations advises next to processes, methods and systems also functions which should get implemented in organisations of service providers. Service Operation processes are Event Management, Incident Management, Problem Management, Request Fulfilment and Access Management. Service Operation functions are Service Desk, Technical Management, IT Operations Management and Application Management. In the following the processes are described from chapter 3.4.1 to 3.4.5. The functions are described from chapter 3.4.6 to 3.4.9.

## 3.4.1 Event Management

ITIL defines an event as *"A change of state that has significance for the management of a Configuration Item or IT Service. The term Event is also used to mean an Alert or notification created by any IT Service, Configuration Item or Monitoring tool. Events typically require IT Operations personnel to take actions, and often lead to Incidents being logged."* (OGC 2007c, p. 232) Event Management is the process that manages all notifications from an IT Service, its CI or a monitoring tool. An event may indicate that something is not functioning correctly, indicate normal activities or a need for routine tasks like changing a tape. Event Management should be applied to any object within Service Management which requires fast control und can be automated with software tools. Events may be classified as:

- Events that indicate a normal operation

- Events that indicate an abnormal operation

- Events that signal an unusual but not exceptional operation

(cf. OGC 2007c, p. 35ff.)

The Event Management activities and the process are shown exemplary in Figure 20.

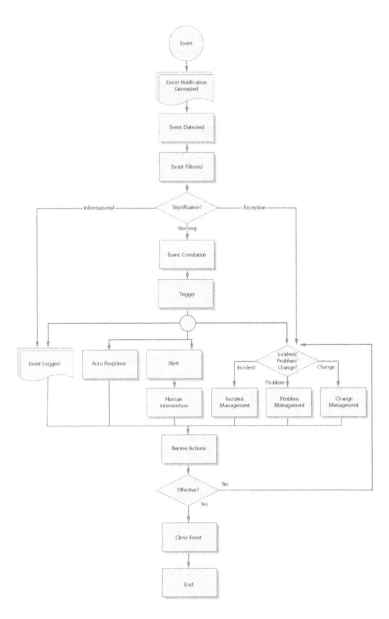

**Figure 20: The Event Management process (OGC 2007c, p. 38)**

## 3.4.2 Incident Management

ITIL defines an incident as *"An unplanned interruption to an IT Service or reduction in the Quality of an IT Service. Failure of a Configuration Item that has not yet affected Service is also an Incident. For example Failure of one disk from a mirror set."* (OGC 2007c, p. 234). All incidents are handled by the Incident Management process. These may be failures or faults that are reported by users or staff members or that are given over by Event Management (see Figure 21, Input interfaces). Basic concepts of Incident Management are:

- Timescales; Time limits for all incident-handling stages generated by SLM.

- Incident models; Pre-defined walkthroughs for handling of standard incidents.

- Impact, urgency, priority; Impact defines the effect of the incident on business. Urgency defines how fast this impact occurs. Priority is category-index for the importance of the incident calculated from impact and urgency.

- Major incidents; An incident with strong impact on the business of the customer. Major incidents require separate procedure with higher urgency.

The Incident management activities and the process are shown exemplary in Figure 21 (cf. OGC 2007c, p. 47ff.).

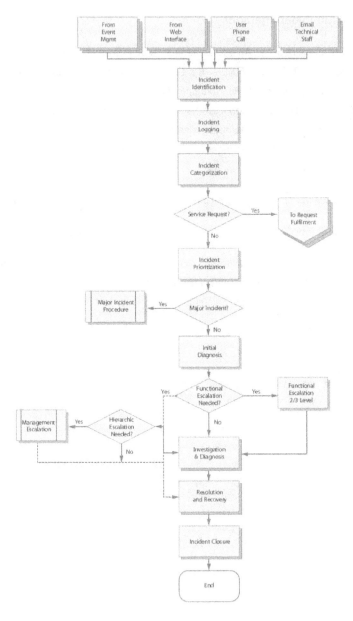

**Figure 21: Incident Management process flow (OGC 2007c, p. 48)**

### 3.4.3 Request Fulfilment

ITIL defines a service request as *"A request from a User for information, or advice, or for a Standard Change or for Access to an IT Service. For example to reset a password, or to provide standard IT Services for a new User. Service Requests are usually handled by a Service Desk, and do not require an RFC to be submitted."* (OGC 2007c, p. 246) A service request is a bit similar to an incident. While incidents (unplanned interruptions) get tracked and dissolved, service requests (small RfCs) get tracked and realised. Service requests changes CIs, but have not been handled by change management (see chapter 3.3.2). The process activities are menu selection, financial authorisation, fulfilment and closure (cf. OGC 2007c, p. 56f.).

### 3.4.4 Problem Management

ITIL defines a problem as *"A cause of one or more Incidents. The cause is not usually known at the time a Problem Record is created, and the Problem Management Process is responsible for further investigation."* (OGC 2007c, p. 240) Incident Management handles all incidents and should fix them expeditiously. In cases of an impossible fixing of the cause, a work around is the solution. Problem management deals inter alia with such incident causes to provide all other processes with workarounds and known errors. The basic concepts are:

- Root cause; Is the fault of an IT Service component (CI) that made the incident occur.

- Workaround; Is a way of eliminating or reducing the impact of an incident for which a solution is not available yet.

- Known error; Is a problem that has a documented root cause and a workaround. All known errors are organised in the known error database (KEDB) which is part of the SKMS (see chapter 3.3.7).

The Problem Management activities and the process are shown exemplary in Figure 22 (cf. OGC 2007c, 58ff.).

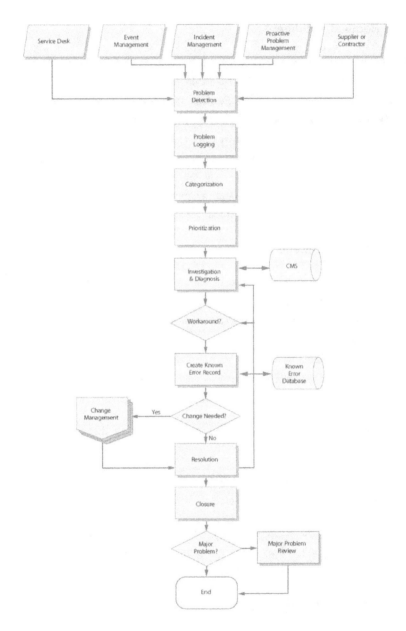

**Figure 22: Problem Management process flow (OGC 2007c, p. 60)**

## 3.4.5 Access Management

Access Management provides and manages all the access rights for users of IT Services or groups of IT Services. This means that access for authorised users is given and access to non-authorised users is prevented. Within some organisations it is also called "rights management" or "identity management". The initiation of Access Management comes inter alia from request fulfilment process. Basic concepts of Access Management are access, identity, rights and IT Service or IT Service group. The main activities are

(1) Requesting access,

(2) Verification,

(3) Granting rights,

(4) Monitoring identity status,

(5) Registering and monitoring access,

(6) Logging and tracking access and

(7) Revoking or limiting rights.

(cf. OGC 2007c, p. 68ff.)

## 3.4.6 Service Desk

Unlike as most of the defined activities by ITIL, the Service Desk and following matters are functions of organisations instead of processes. In case of implementation of it into a service provider's organisation the structural organisation has to be changed. The Service Desk is a functional unit which acts a single point of contact to users. Single point does not mean technical restrictions, communications channel could be phone, email, in person etc. The Service Desk is chiefly the first stage for incident and request fulfilment processes (cf. OGC 2007c, p. 109ff.).

ITnx

Service Desk organisational structures could be:

- Local Service Desk; In the case of distributed locations of the customer, local sites could be provided with a local Service Desk.

- Centralised Service Desk; Is the opposite of the local Service Desk structure. One Service Desk is installed centrally. Advantage at this is an efficient usage of processes and short communication. Disadvantage is that local circumstances, cultural differences, different languages and different time zones could cause troubles.

- Virtual Service Desk; Is the impression of a centralised Service Desk while the associates are spread out over a number of geographic or structural locations. This could be done by using very highly communication technology and supporting tools.

- Follow-the-sun service; Multiple Service Desk are located in different time zones and combined to offer a 24/7 service[1].

- Specialised Service Desk groups; A specific IT Service related incident maybe routed straight to the specialised group.

(cf. OGC 2007c, p. 111ff.)

Main activities of the Service Desk are

(1) Logging all incidents and service requests with corresponding details,

(2) Providing first-line investigation and diagnosis,

(3) Resolving incidents and service requests,

(4) Escalating incidents and service requests which could not get resolved by themselves within timescale (see chapter 3.4.2),

(5) Informing users about the progress,

---

[1] 24/7 means 24 hours per day and 7 days a week thus full time service.

(6) Closing of all incidents and service requests and other calls and

(7) Updating the CMS under the direction and approval of service asset and configuration management.

(cf. OGC 2007c, p. 110)

### 3.4.7 Technical Management

Technical Management plans, implements and maintains the technical infrastructure and provides necessary resources and expertise for design, build, transition, operating and improving the IT Services and supporting technology. The main activities of technical management are

(1) Identifying knowledge and expertise requirements,

(2) Defining architecture standards,

(3) Involvement in design and build of new services and operational practices and

(4) Contribution to all service lifecycle stages.

(cf. OGC 2007c, p. 121ff.)

### 3.4.8 Application Management

Application Management is similar to Technical Management (see chapter 3.4.7) but with the responsibility for applications and software instead of infrastructure matters (cf. OGC 2007c, p. 128).

### 3.4.9 IT Operations Management

Technical and Application Management attend to the management of infrastructure, application and software issues induced by activities of the service lifecycle stages. IT operations management is focused on the range of IT Service operation tasks which ensures the day-to-day delivery of actual IT Services. As the basic concept of IT operations management the Operations Bridge is a central point of coordination. It manages various events and routine operational activities and reports the state and performance of the different IT Service components. It combines activities such as console management, event handling and support outside office hours. In some organisations the Service Desk (see chapter 3.4.6) is part of the operations bridge (cf. OGC 2007c, p. 125ff.).

## 3.5 Continual Service Improvement

All ITIL lifecycle stages as yet described are more or less serial. The handover from Service Strategy to Design to Transition and to Operations are described for each stage in form of service level packages or service packages. Continual Service Improvement (CSI) bridges the lifecycle by improving:

- Process compliance; Does the staff members follows the existing, new or modified processes?

- Quality; Does the process meet it's goals, is it effective?

- Performance; Is the process efficient?

- Business value of a process; Does the process make a difference?

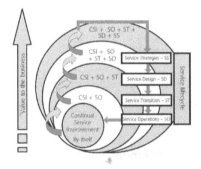

**Figure 23: Bernard-Doppler service improvement levels of opportunity (OGC 2007a, p. 24)**

CSI will not be able to improve the listed matters above on its own. Therefore it is essential to leverage the following processes at each stage of the lifecycle. The expansion of CSI over the other lifecycle stages increases the value to business (see chapter 3.1) as shown in Figure 23 (cf. OGC 2007a, p. 14ff.).

The key processes of CSI are the 7-Step Improvement Process, Service Reporting and Service Measurement.

## 3.5.1 The 7-Step Improvement Process

This process describes how to measure and report on service improvement. This process is closely aligned to the PDCA cycle[2] by Deming. It covers the steps for collecting data, analysing data for trend lining and improvement implementations (see Figure 24).

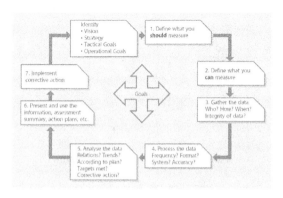

**Figure 24: 7-Step Improvement Process (OGC 2007a, p. 43)**

The 7-Step Improvement process activities are:

(1) What should you measure? Answering the question, what would be the ideal situation? Making a list of what should be measured, should be driven by business requirements. Therefore it is essential not to cover every single eventuality in the world. Keep it simple. According to that, analysis of a corporate vision, mission, goals and objectives and accordingly IT vision, critical success factors and service level targets could answer that question.

(2) What can you measure? By researching what the service provider's organisation can measure, it will discover new business requirements and new

---

[2] PDCA stands for Plan-Do-Check-Act. It is an iterative problem solving process, developed by William Edwards Deming.

IT options. By using a gap analysis CSI can find areas for improvement and plan these.

(3) Gather data (measure); This activity covers monitoring and data collection. A combination of monitoring tools and manual processes should be in place.

(4) Process data; Preparation of data appropriate to each audience.

(5) Analyse data; Data analysis transforms the information into knowledge (see chapter 3.3.7) of the events that are affecting the organisation.

(6) Present and use information; The stake-holder is informed whether the goals have been achieved or not.

(7) Implement corrective action; Creation of improvement measures and start of the 7-Step improvement process again.

(cf. OGC 2007a, p. 43ff.)

How to come from vision to measurement is shown in Figure 25.

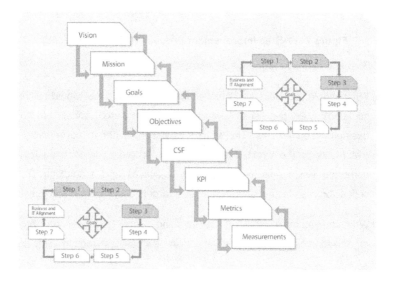

**Figure 25: From vision to measurement (OGC 2007a, p. 48)**

## 3.5.2 Service Measurement

Monitoring and measurement supports CSI and the 7-Step Improvement process. Instead of measuring at the component level, service measurement must go up a level to provide a view of the real customer experience of services being delivered. ITIL recommends distinguishing the metrics which should be measured among three types of

- Technology metrics,

- Process metrics and

- Service metrics.

An integrated service measurement framework gives aid to detect relations and dependencies between them and supports the data collection and reporting of information (cf. OGC 2007a, p. 66ff.).

## 3.5.3 Service Reporting

Service Reporting process reports achieved results and the progress of CSI measures. As basic concept a reporting framework should be established to distinguish the service provider's reports between audience and purpose (cf. OGC 2007a, p. 65).

# 4 Experiences of SMBs with ITIL framework

The ITIL framework as described in chapter 3 is the basic information for drafting an implementation plan. To tailor such a plan to SMBs, their basic and essential needs and requirements should get considered and understood as a majoritarian input. On one hand public available surveys about this topic are often for ITIL framework in version 2 or on the other hand not as suitable as major origin for this master thesis. So I decided to accomplish a survey for elicitation of information and complete the conclusion of this chapter with public information if it is instrumental.

Therefore I distributed a questionnaire (see Appendix A) across contact possibilities on business relevant social websites[3] as well as direct via email to an SMB specific distribution list[4]. The questionnaire was distributed approximately 15.000 times thereby in the Austrian SMB environment during 86 responses. Having regard to the defined restrictions for SMBs and a completed form, 46 responses have been included for this master thesis.

**Definition of an SMB**

The European Union (EU) issued in 2003 an official gazette in which a recommendation by the European Commission relating to definition of SMB is enunciated. The decision criteria are the number of employees and financial thresholds.

- Less than 250 employees and

- an annual sales of 50 millions of Euros at most or

- an annual balance sheet in total of 43 millions of Euros at most.

(cf. Amtsblatt der Europäischen Union 2003, p.4)

---

[3] www.xing.com
[4] Herold Marketing CD, status January 2001. Selection of contact email addresses according to SMB specific selection criteria (see Amtsblatt der Europäischen Union 2003, p. 4)

## 4.1 Structure of the questionnaire

The questionnaire's remit was to capture the given situation and experiences with ITIL framework of SMBs. Therefore the following question blocks were formulated:

- Questions about business in general; To recognise the SMB character of businesses which answered the survey, questions regarding the employee count, annual sales and annual balance sheet in total have to be answered. Basic information about cost spending for IT in total and relative to business overall costs as well as the branch of economy were also levied.

- Questions about the organisational form and level of maturity of the SMB; To interpret the valence of participators answers, its maturity level concerning organisational development and possible management system certifications were enquired.

- Questions about the implementation and experience with ITIL and other Service Management publications; The third question block covers the field of experience with ITIL framework implementation from a qualitative and financial aspect. This ranges from experiences with external consultants to implementation reasons.

## 4.2 Method of data aggregation

The range of thresholds in defining of SMBs is wide having regard to the 46 responses of the sent out questionnaires. The employee count is more important to build peer groups for further statistic analysis of survey results than the financial figures. Depending on the employee count the spent resources for Service Management effort next to operational tasks can be compared. Table 1 shows how the 46 completed forms are distributed over five clusters which are the peer groups for following statistic analysis. All further statistic conclusions are averaged values unless otherwise noted and bases on these peer groups. The figures are in total or relative and rounded to none or one decimal place.

| Peer group | A | B | C | D | E |
|---|---|---|---|---|---|
| Employee count clusters | 1 – 10 | 11 – 50 | 51 – 100 | 101 – 150 | 151 - 250 |
| Average employee count | 3,7 | 39,3 | 59,4 | 113,8 | 159 |
| Completed forms in total | 3 | 6 | 5 | 21 | 11 |
| Completed forms relatively | 6,5% | 13 % | 10,9% | 45,7% | 23,9% |

**Table 1: Peer groups (own illustration 2009, cf. Appendix A, question 1.a)**

45% of all participants form peer group D which is therewith the biggest peer group of all with an average employee account of 113,76.

## 4.3 Statistic conclusions about business in general

Another topic in the questionnaire was of the branch of economic activity as defined by the Austrian federal economic chamber (Wirtschaftskammer Österreich WKO) in it's statistic system called Österreich Nomenclature statistique des activités économiques dans la Communauté européenne (ÖNACE) in version 2008[5] (cf. Statistik Austria 2009). The participants of the survey are dispersed as described in Table 2. Not all branches as defined in ÖNACE are listed in Table 2, only these for which answered questionnaires exist.

---

[5] ÖNACE in version 2008 is the Austrian specification of the European Union (EU) branche classification Nomenclature statistique des activités économiques dans la Communauté européenne (NACE) which is obligatory for Austrias economy since its membership in the EU in 1995.

| Branche \ Peer group | A | B | C | D | E | In total |
|---|---|---|---|---|---|---|
| BAU | - | 1 | 2 | 5 | 1 | 9 |
| BEHERBERGUNG UND GASTRONOMIE | - | 2 | - | - | - | 2 |
| ERBRINGUNG VON SONSTIGEN WIRTSCHAFTLICHEN DIENSTLEISTUNGEN | 2 | - | - | 1 | - | 3 |
| HANDEL; INSTANDHALTUNG UND REPARATUR VON KRAFTFAHRZEUGEN | - | 2 | 2 | 6 | 4 | 14 |
| HERSTELLUNG VON WAREN | - | 1 | - | 6 | 5 | 12 |
| LAND- UND FORSTWIRTSCHAFT; FISCHEREI | 1 | - | - | - | - | 1 |
| VERKEHR UND LAGEREI | - | - | 1 | 3 | 1 | 5 |
| In total | 3 | 6 | 5 | 21 | 11 | |

**Table 2: Number of valid forms based on questionnaire (own illustration 2009, cf. Appendix A, question 1.h)**

It is important to know how staff members are dispersed over IT and non-IT functions within the SMB and also how many of them are SMB internal employed or hired by contract for work and labour. This information and also information about dispersion over different roles in the business allows conclusions about the scale of ITIL framework implementation at SMBs as described in chapter 5.3.3. Table 3 shows how the given organisations of SMBs are setup. For cushy calculation the number of staff members is defined as full time equivalent (FTE)[6].

[6] An FTE is a quantity in the field of human resource planning and budgeting. Business defines the possible average person day utilisation per year (e.g. 240 person days per year are one FTE).

| Dispersion of staff members | Peer group | A | B | C | D | E |
|---|---|---|---|---|---|---|
| FTEs who are responsible for IT and internal employed | In total | 0 | 2,4 | 4,8 | 13,2 | 16,8 |
| | In relation to average employee count | 0,0% | 6,2% | 8,0% | 11,6% | 10,6% |
| FTEs who are responsible for IT and hired by contract for work and labour | In total | 0,1 | 1,4 | 4,9 | 8,7 | 10,7 |
| | In relation to average employee count | 3,6% | 3,7% | 8,2% | 7,7% | 6,7% |
| Sum of FTEs who are responsible for IT | In total | 0,1 | 3,9 | 9,7 | 21,9 | 27,5 |
| | In relation to average employee count | 3,6% | 9,9% | 16,3% | 19,3% | 17,3% |
| FTEs who are responsible for IT and | take charge of management responsibilities (relative against sum of FTEs who are responsible for IT) | 0% | 13% | 13% | 14% | 16% |
| | take charge of business analysis responsibilities (relative against sum of FTEs who are responsible for IT) | 0% | 11% | 25% | 15% | 19% |
| | take charge of software development responsibilities (relative against sum of FTEs who are responsible for IT) | 0% | 5% | 9% | 6% | 14% |
| | take charge of IT operations responsibilities (relative against sum of FTEs who are responsible for IT) | 100% | 71% | 53% | 65% | 51% |

**Table 3: Dispersion of staff members who are responsible for IT within an SMB**

**(own illustration 2009, cf. Appendix A, question 1.b, 1.c, 1.g)**

ITIL framework implementation does not spend efficiency by its own in principle. Contrariwise it costs money but with valuable ITIL framework implementations SMB gets the transparency and controlling mechanism to manage efficiency by processes. Those participating SMBs which have experience with full or partly ITIL framework implementation have an IT cost situation as described in Table 4. How far the efficiency potential of ITIL framework implementation is, is described in chapter 4.5.

| IT costs \ Peer group | | A | B | C | D | E |
|---|---|---|---|---|---|---|
| IT costs in relation to SMBs total costs | | 0,8% | 12,9% | 12,9% | 12,3% | 17,2% |
| Breakdown of IT costs | IT operations costs | 100% | 96,0% | 79,9% | 84,0% | 78,2% |
| | IT innovations costs | 0% | 4,0% | 20,1% | 16,0% | 21,8% |

**Table 4: IT costs and cost spending of participating SMBs (own illustration 2009, cf. Appendix A, question 1.e, 1.f)**

The most strongly represented branches are trading, motorcar repairing and production at peer group D. Participants of this peer group spend most personal effort on IT in relation to other peer groups with 21.9 FTEs, but have next to the unrepresentable peer group A the lowest IT costs in relation to SMBs total costs. Peer group D also has the most participators (see Table 1) which allow the conclusion that participants of this peer group do have the biggest experience with ITIL framework and its application (most staff members, lowest IT costs).

# 4.4 Statistic conclusions about level of organisational maturity

Conclusions of chapter 4.3 are the business frame conditions of SMBs and the weighting of peer group D members. The level of organisational maturity of participating SMBs is an important evidence of motivation and capability to understand the accurate implementation and its vantages. The question was how well is the given organisational structure known and documented. Table 5 shows that members of peer group D have most of the highest maturity level answers selected during the first self assessment part of the questionnaire.

| Self assessment | Peer group | A | B | C | D | E |
|---|---|---|---|---|---|---|
| Functional organisation | Yes, but not documented | 3 | 6 | 2 | 0 | 0 |
| | Yes, but not actually documented at all times | 0 | 0 | 2 | 5 | 2 |
| | Yes, and well documented | 0 | 0 | 1 | 16 | 9 |
| Process organisation | Yes but not documented | 0 | 6 | 2 | 5 | 0 |
| | Yes, but not actually documented at all times | 0 | 0 | 0 | 6 | 6 |
| | Yes and well documented | 0 | 0 | 3 | 10 | 5 |

**Table 5: Self assessment of participating SMBs regarding organisational structure (own illustration 2009, cf. Appendix A, question 2.a, 2.b)**

The second self assessment part asked about the maturity of SMBs business processes and offered 5 possible levels of maturity to select. These 5 levels of maturity were defined in the questionnaire as:

1. Initial; Processes are not defined; schedules, deliverables and costs are not predictable and measureable.

2. Managed; Processes are known and managed. Connatural processes are repeatable.

3. Defined; Processes are known and documented. Process roles are known and documented. A continuous improvement process (CIP) is implemented.

4. Quantitatively managed; Maturity level "defined" and a verifiable statistic process monitoring is done.

5. Optimizing; Maturity level "quantitatively managed" and the processes become verifiable improved by the statistic process monitoring.

Table 6 shows the result of the self assessment.

| Maturity level \ Peer group | A | B | C | D | E | In total |
|---|---|---|---|---|---|---|
| 1, Initial | 0 | 0 | 0 | 0 | 0 | 0 |
| 2, Managed | 0 | 0 | 0 | 2 | 2 | 4 |
| 3, Defined | 0 | 1 | 0 | 12 | 7 | 20 |
| 4, Quantitatively managed | 0 | 0 | 2 | 6 | 2 | 10 |
| 5, Optimising | 0 | 0 | 1 | 0 | 0 | 1 |
| No selection | 3 | 5 | 2 | 1 | 0 | 11 |
| In total | 3 | 6 | 5 | 21 | 11 | |

**Table 6: Self assessment of participating SMBs regarding business process maturity level (own illustration 2009, cf. Appendix A, question 2.c)**

The last question of the self assessment was about the state of organisational setup of business. Possible answers to select were: functional organised, process organised or matrix organisation. Table 7 shows the answers of the peer group members.

| Organisational form \ Peer group | A | B | C | D | E | In total |
|---|---|---|---|---|---|---|
| Functional organisation | 0 | 4 | 1 | 4 | 0 | 9 |
| Process organisation | 0 | 0 | 0 | 0 | 0 | 0 |
| Matrix organisation | 0 | 0 | 3 | 17 | 11 | 31 |
| No selection | 3 | 2 | 1 | 0 | 0 | 6 |
| In total | 3 | 6 | 5 | 21 | 11 | |

**Table 7: Self assessment of participating SMBs regarding organisational setup (own illustration 2009, cf. Appendix A, question 2.d)**

The known and well documented functional and process organisation was selected most times by peer group D members who also have most selections at the maturity level question. With twelve of 20 selections of maturity level 3, the first level with most participators is reached which ensures a CIP; the precious basic for ITIL framework implementation. The matrix organisation essential for ITIL framework implementation is selected most times by peer group D members.

## 4.5 Statistic conclusions about ITIL implementation and experiences

Based on the positioning as the most representative peer group, the statements and statistic conclusions of peer group D members are used as basis for analysing the experiences of SMBs with ITIL framework. This decision shall be fortified by the statistic conclusions about experiences with ITIL framework implementations. Table 8 gives an impression of the organisational change concept (see chapter 5.1) used by SMBs to implement ITIL framework in their organisational environment. Thrice as much times the organisational approach was selected next to the Business Reengineering approach.

| Peer group / Organisational change concept | A | B | C | D | E | In total |
|---|---|---|---|---|---|---|
| Business Reenginering | 0 | 0 | 0 | 4 | 2 | 6 |
| Organisational Development | 0 | 1 | 3 | 15 | 7 | 26 |
| No selection | 3 | 5 | 2 | 2 | 2 | 14 |
| In total | 3 | 6 | 5 | 21 | 11 | |

**Table 8: Application of organisational change concepts by SMBs (own illustration 2009, cf. Appendix A, question 3.a)**

The impact of the functional organisation on ITIL process framework implementation was perceived by members of peer groups C to E during their activities with ITIL. How far this impact goes is described in chapter 5.3.3. The most changes of functional organisation were done by peer group D members in relation to non-change as pointed out in Table 9.

| Change of functional organisation \ Peer group | A | B | C | D | E | In total |
|---|---|---|---|---|---|---|
| Change of functional organisation | 0 | 0 | 1 | 12 | 3 | 16 |
| No change of functional organisation | 0 | 1 | 2 | 7 | 6 | 16 |
| No selection | 3 | 5 | 2 | 2 | 2 | 14 |
| In total | 3 | 6 | 5 | 21 | 11 | |

**Table 9: Change of functional organisation during ITIL framework implementation by SMBs (own illustration 2009, cf. Appendix A, question 3.b)**

The method to execute an organisational change is a healthy success criterion of effectiveness. CIP is a method that needs more time than Evaluation although the outcome is embedded more strongly than by Evaluation. The result as shown in Table 10 does not amaze due to the figures of Table 8. As described in chapter 5, organisational change concept uses CIP in the main as well as Business Reengineering uses Evaluation mostly. Capability Maturity Model Integration (CMMI) is used secondly mostly although it is strongly focused on only technical processes (see chapter 5.3).

| Organisational change method \ Peer group | A | B | C | D | E | In total |
|---|---|---|---|---|---|---|
| CIP | 0 | 0 | 2 | 9 | 6 | 17 |
| CMMI[7] | 0 | 1 | 2 | 8 | 1 | 12 |
| Evaluation | 0 | 0 | 0 | 4 | 2 | 6 |
| No selection | 3 | 5 | 1 | 0 | 2 | 11 |
| In total | 3 | 6 | 5 | 21 | 11 | |

**Table 10: Organisational change methods which were used by SMBs to implement ITIL framework (own illustration 2009, cf. Appendix A, question 3.c)**

---

[7] see chapter 5.3

While all previous questions deal with information about SMBs and ITIL framework methods and concepts, the subject-matter of question illustrated in Table 11 represents the reason for ITIL framework implementation. To obtain a comparable result for such question it is necessary to prepare an adequate structure. ITIL framework in version 3 provides a set of processes structured in five service lifecycle stages which aim five purposes. To improve

- Finance,

- Functionality,

- Quality

- Strategy and

- Transparency

of the provided services. The corresponding question in the questionnaire was to select which of these service characteristics were the initialised reason for ITIL framework implementation. The participant's answers are shown in Table 11.

| Service characteristics / Peer group | A | B | C | D | E | In total |
|---|---|---|---|---|---|---|
| Financial | 0 | 0 | 0 | 2 | 3 | 5 |
| Functionality | 0 | 1 | 2 | 4 | 0 | 7 |
| Quality | 0 | 0 | 0 | 5 | 3 | 8 |
| Strategic | 0 | 0 | 1 | 3 | 1 | 5 |
| Transparency | 0 | 0 | 0 | 5 | 2 | 7 |
| No selection | 3 | 5 | 2 | 2 | 2 | 14 |
| In total | 3 | 6 | 5 | 21 | 11 | |

**Table 11: Reasons for ITIL framework implementation (own illustration 2009, cf. Appendix A, question 3.d)**

The last question in the questionnaire was prepared with three assumption scenarios and the request to answer in respect to the given structure based on SMBs experiences over time with ITIL framework in version 2 and/or 3. The result was a combination of ITIL processes and functions in work packages which are easier and more efficient to implement correspondingly under consideration of the aim of processes. The three assumption scenarios were:

- An In-house IT department, cost centre, with legacy systems in the main implements ITIL framework in version 3.

- An In-house IT department, cost centre, with standard software (partly outtasked) in the main implements ITIL framework in version 3.

- An In-house or outsourced IT department, cost or profit centre, with legacy systems or standard software implements ITIL framework in version 3.

Within the given structure all ITIL processes and functions of version 3 were listed with an adequate match to ITIL processes and functions in version 2 if applicable. This match advances the possibility for participants to answer with their long time experience with ITIL due to the short time ITIL in version 3 is released. To have one consistent basis for the efficient holistic implementation plan, the recommendations of conclusions of chapter 4.3 and 4.4 are considered to that effect that only the result of peer group D is shown in Table 12 and used for the holistic efficient implementation plan.

The participator was requested to recommend a work package structure per assumption scenario for correspondingly clustering ITIL processes. In Table 12 the right three headers name the assumption scenarios and in the subjacent two columns is given the number of work packages and how often it was selected in percentage points. For example: 19 of the 21 peer group D members selected incident management for work package 1, it becomes listed with number 1 and 90%.

For only more than 30% of same selections of one process or function with the same recommended work package number has been given thought to.

| ITIL framework in version 3 | Process or function in version 3 | Process or function in version 2 | In-house IT department, cost centre, with legacy systems in the main | | In-house IT department, cost centre, with standard software (partly outtasked) in the main | | In-house or outsourced IT department, cost or profit centre, with legacy systems or standard software | |
|---|---|---|---|---|---|---|---|---|
| Service Strategy | Demand Management | Capacity Management | - | - | - | - | 1 | 38% |
| Service Strategy | Financial Management | Financial Management for IT-Services | - | - | - | - | 1 | 49% |
| Service Strategy | Service Portfolio Management | - | - | - | - | - | - | - |
| Service Strategy | Strategy Generation | - | - | - | - | - | - | - |
| Service Design | Availability Management | Availability Management | 3 | 35% | 4 | 38% | 3 | 56% |
| Service Design | Capacity Management | Capacity Management | - | - | 4 | 32% | 3 | 56% |
| Service Design | Information Security Management | Security Management | ongoing | 30% | ongoing | 32% | ongoing | 42% |
| Service Design | IT Service Continuity Management | IT Service Continuity Management | 3 | 33% | 4 | 28% | 3 | 61% |
| Service Design | Service Catalogue Management | Service Level Management | - | - | - | - | 1 | 56% |
| Service Design | Service Level Management | Service Level Management | - | - | 3 | 46% | 4 | 74% |
| Service Design | Supplier Management | - | - | - | 3 | 82% | 4 | 58% |
| Service Transition | Change Management | Change Management | 2 | 67% | 2 | 78% | 2 | 76% |
| Service Transition | Evaluation | - | - | - | - | - | - | - |
| Service Transition | Knowledge Management | - | - | - | - | - | 5 | 32% |
| Service Transition | Release and Deployment Management | Release Management, Deployment Management | 2 | 59% | 2 | 52% | 2 | 71% |
| Service Transition | Service Asset and Configuration Management | Configuration Management | 2 | 67% | 2 | 78% | 2 | 76% |
| Service Transition | Service Validation and Testing | - | - | - | - | - | 2 | 61% |
| Service Transition | Transition Planning and Support | - | 2 | 47% | 2 | 36% | 2 | 67% |
| Service Operation | Access Management | - | - | - | - | - | - | - |
| Service Operation | Event Management | Incident Management | - | - | - | - | 5 | 86% |
| Service Operation | Function: Application Management | Application Management | - | - | - | - | - | - |
| Service Operation | Function: IT Operations Management | Operations | - | - | - | - | - | - |
| Service Operation | Function: Service Desk | Function: Service Desk | - | - | - | - | - | - |
| Service Operation | Function: Technical Management | Technical Support | - | - | - | - | - | - |
| Service Operation | Incident Management | Incident Management | 1 | 90% | 1 | 87% | 5 | 86% |
| Service Operation | Problem Management | Problem Management | - | - | 1 | 52% | 5 | 84% |
| Service Operation | Request Fulfilment | Incident Management | - | - | 1 | 87% | 5 | 86% |
| Continual Service Improvement | Business Questions for CSI | - | - | - | - | - | - | - |
| Continual Service Improvement | Service Measurement | - | - | - | 3 | 46% | 4 | 74% |
| Continual Service Improvement | Return on Investment for CSI | - | - | - | - | - | - | - |
| Continual Service Improvement | Service Reporting | Service Level Management | - | - | 3 | 46% | 4 | 74% |
| Continual Service Improvement | The 7-Step Improvement Process | - | - | - | - | - | 1 | 34% |

Table 12: ITIL framework clustering (own illustration 2009, cf. Appendix A, question 3.e, 3.f, 3.g)

# 5 An efficient holistic implementation plan

This chapter describes the way how to implement the recommendations of ITIL in a manner that all surrounding conditions are considered. It is important to set a target and a need for ITIL implementation otherwise the risk occurs that ITIL comes for its own sake. Service Management is a useful management system if the organisation concerned really has a need for it. This need results mainly from weak quality of provided IT, unsatisfied customers, sourcing pretensions, etc. The Evaluation of nominal state as well as the setup of an organisational change project ensures that such baseline for an ITIL implementation including vision and consideration of strategy is rightly acquired.

How far ITIL is implemented depends on the target. For example, if one only needs to improve his/her support capabilities, the implementation of an IT-Service Catalogue is not as expedient as the implementation of an incident management process. Otherwise if you plan to organise the complete IT department of an SMB as a service or profit centre you should implement a management system which allows Service Management with a high quality attitude and economic methods like portfolio and financial management.

As described in chapter 3, ITIL is a management system in its entirety with a lot of methods for the different stages of an IT-Service lifecycle. These methods are mainly processes, plans, concepts and principles and marginally approach for databases or systems. Implementation of ITIL is therefrom not a typical IT project for soft- or hardware. It is an organisational change with all the typical characteristics for this kind of project. If a service provider decides to implement the whole ITIL management system for Service Management for example, the major tasks are implementing new processes, abandon existing processes and change the functional organisation structure. As a matter of course necessary support tools like an incident management tool or database solutions are near by but always follow the needs of the processes.

Considering that, an efficient holistic implementation of ITIL calls for preoccupation with planned organisational changes and due consideration of target and nominal state of the implementation. That assures optimum quality of implementation. Following is described:

- which concepts of planned organisational changes are available,

- how the nominal state could be evaluated and

- which topics have to be covered by an ITIL implementation project.

## 5.1 Concepts of planned organisational change

A business has to organise itself by division of labour. This is necessary to achieve an overall task; each participating person has to cover parts of this task. Jean Paul Thommen[8] defines the task of an organisation as *"Organisieren bedeutet, die Gesamtaufgabe des Unternehmens, die von Menschen und Maschinen arbeitsteilig erfüllt werden muss, sinnvoll in Teilaufgaben zu gliedern und diese zueinander in Beziehung zu setzen, damit die Ziele des Unternehmens optimal erreicht werden."* (Thommen et al 2003, p. 742) He describes that, organising is to divide expediently the overall task of a business in correlated subtasks in respect of ideal achieving business objectives. The term **organisation** is used for different meaning in the field of economics and colloquially. From an economics point of view the following interpretations come to the fore:

- Formative aspect; The business **will be** organised. The task of creation comes to the fore by this aspect thus organisation is a **formative function**.

- Regulative aspect; The business **has an** organisation. This aspect relies on a general rule which says each business has a created cognisant system for achieving certain goals. This system bears on the structures and

---

[8] Jean Paul Thommen holds the professorship for business studies, particularly labour and organisation, at the European Business School (ebs) Schloss Reichartshausen and is Lecturer at the University of St. Gallen and Zurich.

processes of business. By this aspect, organisation is a **regulation function**.

• Institutional aspect; The business **is an** organisation.

(cf. Thommen et al 2003, p. 742f.)

Within this chapter the formative aspect gets described because the implementation of ITIL is mainly a change of the organisation. If the management of a business decides that the internal service provider has to change from Systems Management to Service Management, the given organisational structure has to be changed. Thommen calls it *"...geplanter organisatorischer Wandel..."* (Thommen et al, 2003, p. 817) which means planed change of the organisation. The most representative concepts for organisational changes are **Business Reengineering** and **Organisational Development**. At Business Reengineering, a team of experts is engaged with reorganizational[9] measures which enable other-determined solutions. At Organisational Development, the affected business internal staff members develop measures on their own to enable self-determined solutions.

The flow chart of Figure 26 describes as a constitutional thinking model, the main activities for a reorganisation respectively new organisation at varying levels of details. The different activities may have various degrees of complexity and novelty. Therefrom dependent certain phases may get consolidated, more detailed or overlapped. These activities are addressed within this chapter to describe which aspects have to be considered and activities have to be done. Phases 1 to 3 are described in chapter 5.3. Phase 4 and 5 are not in the focus of this master thesis since they are too specific for different businesses.

(cf. Thommen et al 2003, p. 817ff.)

---

[9] *„Mit Reorganisation oder Restrukturierung wird im allgemeinen die Veränderung der Unternehmensorganisation, speziell der Aufbauorganisation bezeichnet. ..."* (Projektmagazin 2009) Reorganisation means change of the organisation of a business, especially the structural organisation.

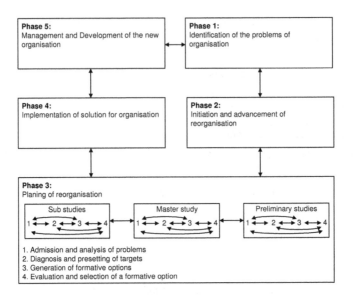

**Figure 26: Activities of a reorganisation process (own illustration 2009,
cf. Thommen et al 2003, p. 818)**

**Phase 1** comprises the identification of problems of the organisation. A problem of organisation is given if organisational rules, which enable efficient task fulfilment, do not come into action any more (e.g. duplication of work, unclear responsibilities). The cause for such problems could be not only a difficulty within the organisation or at its context. It could also be a change of business objectives, new vision or mission, ethic aspects or growth of the business.

**Phase 2** enables the formative process from a formal perspective since identifying problems of the organisation ensures this not necessarily. On the one hand, all the necessary contributions and costs have to be pondered because all costs and consequential costs of a reorganisation project should not exceed the expected benefits. On the other hand, all possible proponents and opponents should get cognised. Impeding and encouraging forces that appear between the problem identification and setup of the reorganisation become manageable and assessable.

During **phase 3**, the reorganisation project planning, the following questions should be clarified:

- Which value should be achieved and for whom?

- Who should be project manager? Therefore back the preparatory operations.

- What is in focus and what not?

- What is the expense of the reorganisation project?

- How shall the organisational change project be implemented?

The general approach should be detailed during the planning phase by breakdown into three parts which differ by their level of detail. These are the preliminary study, master study and sub study.

- The result of the **preliminary study** could be a rough tendency for solution.

- The **master study** builds solution concepts based on the rough tendency. The whole problem gets divided into determined problem areas.

- Feasible implementation plans are elaborated from the problem areas by several **sub studies**.

(cf. Thommen et al 2003, p. 819f.)

## 5.1.1 Business Reengineering

*"Business Reengineering bedeutet ein fundamentals Überdenken und radikales Redesign von Unternehmen oder wesentlichen Unternehmensprozessen. Das Resultat sind außerordentliche Verbesserungen und entscheidenden, heute wichtigen und messbaren Leistungsgrößen in den Bereichen Kosten, Qualität, Service und Zeit."* (Hammer et al 1994, p. 48)

Michael Hammer[10] as a founder of Business Reengineering describes it as a fundamental and extreme redesign of business or important business processes. The outcomes are exceeding and measurable improvements in the field of costs, quality, services and time. Fundamental and extreme means always the question "**What?**" that is to say, what are important tasks of a business? To achieve the defined objective of a reorganisational measure, the existing organisational structure or processes do not get adapted but designed completely new. The main focus of attention hereby lies at the core processes of the value-added chain. In short terms: Don't adapt, make it new (cf. Thommen et al 2003, p. 822f.).

## 5.1.2 Organisational Development

Changes of organisation mostly encounter resistance of staff members. Resistance has to be seen as a matter of course by changes or innovations and results by concern of affected people. This concern bases on the fear that disadvantages appear compared with the given situation. Information is partly an appropriate means against such resistance and so it is recommended, that the reason of the change and the final state are described and disclosed. The progress should be reported during the change process. As another solution people concerned shall participate in the change process as put into effect in the concept of organisational development. Thereby involved people get a chance to tamper with the process as well as the result.

Organisational Development was developed in the 1940s by social psychologist as a form of planned change of the organisation to achieve better efficiency of organisation (economical objectives) as well as origination of potential for individual gratification (individual-social objectives). Organisational Development is a long-term improvement and change process and bases on learning of all concerned people by contribution and practical experience. The aim is to improve the productivity (effectiveness) and the quality of working life (humanity) contemporaneously.

---

[10] Michael Hammer was an author and former professor at the Massachusetts Institute of Technology (MIT) and is deemed to be a founder of the management theory of Business Process Engineering.

Three elementary principles for application are:

- **Making involved out of concerned people**; Those who have to work aligned with new rules have to be involved by their formulation.

- **Helping people help themselves**; Involved people define the content of the reorganisation supported by consultants on their own.

- **Compensation of power**; The value of democratisation and dehierarchisation of working life is closely connected with the two above listed basic values.

(cf. Thommen et al 2003, p. 824, Schanz 1982, p. 329ff.)

A popular phase breakdown model for the change process comes from Kurt Lewin[11] which defines three main phases as shown in Figure 27.

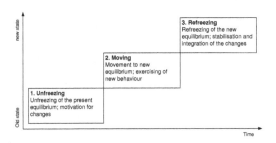

**Figure 27: Three-stage model of the change process (own illustration 2009, Kiechl 1995, p. 291)**

## 5.1.3 Comparison of Business Reengineering and Organisational Development

The following table compiles basic information, characteristics and strengths and weaknesses of Business Reengineering and Organisational Development and compare them to each other.

---

[11] Kurt Zadek Lewin was one of the first researchers who studied organisational development.

| | Business Reengineering | Organisational Development |
|---|---|---|
| Origin of approaches | • Engineering sciences/ Consulting practice (Management oriented) | • Social psychology/ Consulting practice (Social oriented) |
| Basic idea | • Fundamental review and extreme redesign of business and business processes (revolutionary change) | • Long-term and organisation-widespread change and improvement process of organisation and involved people (evolutionary change) |
| Normative basic position (choices) | • Discontinuous thinking<br>• Ask why?<br>• Making involved out of convinced people | • Making involved out of concerned people<br>• Helping people help themselves<br>• Compensation of power |
| Characterisation of change | • Profound and widespread change<br>• Discontinuity<br>• Change by larger thrusts | • Durable learn and improvement process<br>• Continuity<br>• Change by small steps |
| Timeframe | • Multiannual with pressure on quick results (measurable) | • Long-term with patience and openness (e.g. self-dynamic) |
| Object for change | • Business as a whole respectively core processes | • Business as a whole respectively parts of it |
| Objectives | • Increase of profitability | • Increase of profitability (economical efficiency) and humanity (social efficiency) |
| Strengths | • Clear determination of change phases<br>• Chance for recommencement<br>• Chance for explicit increase of profitability<br>• Quickness of change<br>• Standardisation of change | • Social sustainability<br>• Natural change<br>• Consideration of developability of involved system members<br>• Encouragement of self-management and self-organisation<br>• Prevention and reduction of resistance |
| Weaknesses | • Instability during the change process<br>• Pressure on time and to act<br>• Pressure on short-term results<br>• Exclusion of alternative change strategies<br>• Wanting social sustainability | • Low reaction rate<br>• Very high demands on social expertise of change manager<br>• Coercion to compromise<br>• Insufficient method for implementation of unpopular but necessary decisions (underestimation of power constituent) |

**Table 13: Comparison of Business Reengineering and Organisational Development (own illustration 2009, cf. Thommen et al 2003, p. 827f.)**

## 5.2 The principle of Evaluation

To ensure that invested effort and budget is well spent, a clear definition of the target state and situation should be defined, just as well a review of the final implemented solution. As mentioned in chapter 4.5, most members of the peer group decided to use a three stage approach for their ITIL implementation:

- Formulation of the aim and target of ITIL implementation.

- Implementing what is formulated.

- Check if the implementation achieves the formulated aim and targets.

This approach is very similar with the one Reinhard Stockmann[12] describes as Evaluation: He defines Evaluation as information retrieval with empirical methods and information valuation with systematically methods. The valuation of circumstances is thereby not done according to defined standards like ISO 9001[13] or European Foundation for Quality Management (EFQM). It is done according to different criteria which focus on the utility of items, circumstances or improvements processes. These criteria get defined by all stake- and shareholders and must be defined at the beginning of the Evaluation. Evaluation accomplishes four interconnected general functions (see Figure 28):

- Awareness of findings and expertise,

- Monitoring,

- Establishment of transparency and conversational opportunities to further developments and

- Legitimating of realised measures.

---

[12] Reinhard Stockmann is a professor for sociology and director of the Center for Evaluation (CEval) at the University of Saarland, Germany.
[13] ISO 9001 is a Quality Management standard of the International Organization for Standardization (ISO).

5 An efficient holistic implementation plan

An Evaluation covers various phases:

- For planning of improvement projects or measures

- For accomplishment

- For effectiveness and sustainability test

An overview of these and the feedback loops between is given in Table 14 (cf. Stockmann 2006, p. 65ff.).

| Phases | Perspective of analysis | Cognisance | Evaluation concept |
|---|---|---|---|
| Planning phase | ex-ante | • Analysis for policy<br>• Science for action | • Performative, formative<br>• Active constitutive<br>• Process oriented<br>• Constructional |
| Accomplishment | on-going | • Either possible | • Formative, summative<br>• Either possible |
| Effectiveness | ex-post | • Analysis of policy<br>• Science for knowledge | • Summative: in summary, balancing, result oriented |

**Table 14: Dimensions of Evaluation research (own illustration 2009, cf. Stockmann 2006, p. 70)**

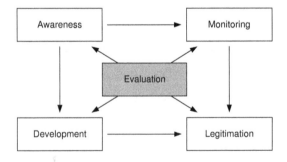

**Figure 28: General functions of Evaluation (own illustration 2009, cf. Stockmann 2006, p. 67)**

The principle of Evaluation is described within this master thesis as a roughly model for understanding how the efficient holistic implementation plan for ITIL framework works. The different steps in the workflow to get the efficient holistic implementation plan, are described in the problem solving process by Thommen in chapter 5.3.2.

## 5.3 The planning phase

Following the Evaluation approach, an as-is analysis should be done within the first efforts of dealing with ITIL framework. Most of the peer group members (see chapter 4.5) decided not do to such analysis, they do it as a continuous improvement process (CIP) or choose the CMMI by the Software Engineering Institute (SEI)[14].

*"Capability Maturity Model® Integration (CMMI) is a process improvement approach that provides organizations with the essential elements of effective processes. It can be used to guide process improvement across a project, a division, or an entire organization. CMMI helps integrate traditionally separate organizational functions, set process improvement goals and priorities, provide guidance for quality processes, and provide a point of reference for appraising current processes."* (SEI 2009b)

Unfortunately CMMI is as it is designed, a process improvement method for software processes primarily. As described in Chapter 3, ITIL is more than that because software design, build and run tasks were split over the different service lifecycle stages as part of the over all management of IT Services. Before ITIL becomes implemented the decision, what it should improve, has to be done for setting objectives. For example, if the analysis phase shows gaps or problems in the area of change management, a process assessment gives a detailed and measurable statement. This assessment should be done along with a reference model like CMMI, especially if more processes are affected or clear defined

---

[14] *„As part of Carnegie Mellon University, [...] The SEI works closely with defense and government organizations, industry, and academia to continually improve our software-intensive systems."* (SEI 2009a)

statements are part of a contract in a project. But, to know that activities are necessary in the area of change management, a more extensive assessment has to be done. The first assessment shall clarify the aim of an ITIL framework implementation and accordingly the details. The planning phase is an ex-ante perspective in an Evaluation process (see Table 14).

ITIL in its entirety affects the functionality and quality of IT providers outcome. It affects the way how IT providers appear against customers and suppliers, it affects how the service of the IT provider is purchased, delivered and charged. Decisions for system or Service Management have to be done as well as sourcing strategies and demand management. It is necessary to know which of the basic questions should be addressed while such analysis phase and which not. To ensure, that everything is considered, the following questions have to be concerned:

- Who are the stake- and shareholders of the IT provider? What are their visions, strategies and how do they affect the IT provider's behaviour?

- What are known actual problems?

- What are well known unsatisfied requirements of customers?

Answering these questions enables focus on essential processes to assess their maturity. Within this chapter, the way how to answer these questions and formulate an efficient holistic implementation plan for ITIL framework is described by the following phases:

- Environment analysis

- Analysis of known, actual problems

- Analysis of well known unsatisfied requirements of customers

- Description of the gaps and subjects of activity

- Definition of the nominal state

## 5.3.1 Environment analysis

Each standard for project management recommends an environment analysis. While management of projects, a lot of interfaces to other tasks and initiatives or projects appear. Also unexpected disturbances make it necessary to cognise, describe and manage different environments. For an implementation plan the environment analysis also identifies potential customers and influencing values. With the aid of a environment analysis the embedding of the ITIL framework implementation is clearly presentable. The aim of the environment analysis is:

- Identification of customers and influencing values

- Identification of dependencies and coherences to other projects or stake- and shareholders

- Identification of possible unexpected disturbances and accordant preparation

Patzak and Rattay[15] recommend the following four step approach for such an analysis:

a) Identification of the project environment means the holistic reflexion and methodical listening of all stake- and shareholders which have influence or dependency on the implementation project. Additionally to the recommendation by Patzak and Rattay a further consideration shall not only focus on the implementation project. It is also necessary to identify the stake- and shareholders for the ongoing ITIL framework in the responsibility of the IT provider. The project environment could be divided into social and factual influencing variables. Social (organisational) variables are supporting or inhibiting and are submitted by several persons, groups of persons or pressure groups. Factual variables are influencing values of

---

[15] Univ.-Prof. Dipl.-Ing. Dr. Gerold Patzak and Dr. Günter Rattay are the autors of „Pojektmanagement". Gerold Patzak is university professor for system technology and methodology an the Technical University of Vienna as well as adjunct Professor at the University of Colorado. Günter Rattay is chairman of Primas CONSULTING, a consulting business for project management, process management and organisational development.

business or customers and are appealed by individual persons (e.g. other projects, laws, technologies, strategies) (cf. Patzak et al 2009, p. 95f.).

b) Structuring of influencing values; The following table gives an overview of typical project environments and influencing variables.

| Type of variable | Business internal or external | Project environment and influencing value |
|---|---|---|
| Social | Internal | • Executive management<br>• Project sponsor and promoter<br>• Project manager<br>• Project team<br>• Departments, business segments, service areas affected by project<br>• Formal decision maker<br>• Informal decision maker and opinion former<br>• Occasional contributors from the business |
| Social | External | • Customers<br>• Sponsors, financiers<br>• Users, Operators<br>• Project team members from customers or suppliers<br>• Supplier<br>• Competitors of business or internal IT department<br>• Public authorities<br>• The media, publicity |
| Factual | internal and external | • Coexistent projects<br>• Routine jobs of business<br>• New technologies<br>• Regulatory requirements<br>• Know-how<br>• Labour market<br>• Economical strategies from business, customers or suppliers |

**Table 15: List of frequently occurring environments and influencing values (own illustration 2009, cf. Patzak et al 2003, p. 97)**

c) Validation of the environment and a detailed analysis; Several stake- and shareholders can have more or less strong influence on and dependency of an implementation. The project manager has to analyse the stake- and shareholders listed in Table 15 with higher impact more in detail than others with lower impact. The following areas of social variables should be reflected and quantitative stated per stake- and shareholder. Is the respective stake- or shareholder positive, negative or ambivalent (neutral) attuned. The point is to identify promoters and opponents of the project (Attitude to project). How strong is the potential power and influence by the respective stake- or shareholder. Strong influence on the ITIL framework implementation connotes that these stake- or shareholders could scupper the reorganisation project or help on (Power, influence). Validation of the possibility that the interests of the respective stake- or shareholder could be antagonistic with the targets of the IITL process framework implementation, independent of the power and influence of the respective stake- or shareholder. The point is to prophylactic concentrate effort on these stake- and shareholders in case of crisis (Conflict potential). All expectations and fears have to be verbal formulated by respective stake- and shareholder. In combination with other variables (e.g. power, influence, and conflict potential) the project manager should respond in an adequate manner (Expectations, fears).

The reflection and quantification of the factual variables should be done in the following areas. For each respective stake- and shareholder the consequences, impact and repercussions on the project and the ITIL framework implementation itself shall be formulated e.g. quality, milestones/dead lines, resources, costs, functionality (Consequences, impact, repercussions). Definition and description of preventive behaviour patterns and solutions based on the earlier mentioned variables (Measures).

(cf. Patzak et al 2009, p. 98ff.)

d) Derivation of measures; The analysis (see chapter 5.3.1c) presents weighted project environment as completely as possible. That is the basis for definition of adequate measures to fulfil requirements and pattern relationships. They could vary in immediate measures and reactive measures and strategies. Immediate measures are coming in effect as soon as necessary. Reactive measures should be defined as soon as possible but come in affect if a specific event occurs. By that a fast and coordinated reaction is possible. Strategies define certain encounter measures and attitudes. Strategies could be distinguished by embedding in the decision-making process, based on partnership (participative approach), discussion of solutions and giving of strategic information. Carrying out of conflicts (discursive approach) or react only on request, confrontation with fait accompli, exercising power (repressive approach). (cf. Patzak et al 2009, p. 103)

## 5.3.2 Analysis of known problems and unsatisfied customer requirements

The principles of Evaluation by Stockmann (see chapter 5.2) describes the main three steps in high level, the problem solving process by Thommen particularises it as shown in Figure 29. Dealing with ITIL framework implementation minds shall always base on reasons for it. If not, the reorganisational project will either be not successfully or for the sake of ITIL. It is very important to understand, which deficits, problems or unsolved customer requests have to be dissolved.

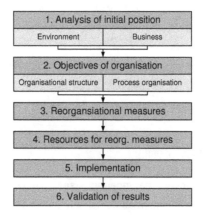

**Figure 29: Problem solving process for reorganisation (own illustration 2009, cf. Thommen et al 2003, p. 745)**

**The first step** in the problem solving process by Thommen is an analysis of the initial position for a possible reorganisation. A multiplicity of influencing factors affects the organisation of a business. ITIL framework implementation is thus also not only a solution for the internal IT department of a business; It is a solution for the whole business and significantly applied in the IT department or by an fully or partly outsourced service provider. The main part of the first step is described in chapter 5.3.1 as the environment analysis. Additionally to this business specific criteria like the extensiveness of the whole enterprise, quantity of products etc. have to be recognised, linked together and formulated (cf. Thommen et al 2003, p. 744). The survey by SMBs as described in chapter 4.5 pointed out the way how SMBs evaluated the initial position. The most important perspectives in which the problems, given conditions and customer requirements were appraised are:

- Strategic evolution of the IT department respectively the purchased service provider (strategy)

- Delivery of automatism and information for customer's business (functionality)

- Agreed quality of provided solutions and ensuring it by regular monitoring and reporting (quality)

- Most possible allocation of costs to provided solutions (financial)

- Near real time information about actual state of incidents and change requests during operation and innovation processes of provided and new solutions (transparency)

These five perspectives shall be the framework for analysis of the initial position for ITIL framework implementation. Contemplating the process of the IT provider in these areas a lot of dependencies become clear. As an example, if the customer requests a very fast response in case of an incident (see chapter 3.4.2), the organisational structure and processes behind have to be designed to ensure that. This is a customer requirement which also generates potentially costs. Therefrom this request influences the perspective of quality and financial. If the customer requests thereunto a daily status report about the progress of the incident, the perspective of transparency is also affected. As another example, if the management of the business decides that the IT department should be fully outsourced in the medium-term, a possible change from cost to profit centre has to be concerned. The perspective of strategy and financial is therefrom affected.

For the first step of the problem solving process and also the ex-ante phase of the Evaluation, a score card (see Figure 30) with these five perspectives and interdependencies between is an adequate tool. It becomes possible to highlight the topics, which areas are affected and all the dependences between. A derivation of one identified topic to another topic in another perspective ensures high quality of problem and unsatisfied customer requirement analysis.

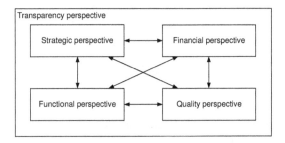

**Figure 30: Perspectives for an analysis of known problems and unsatisfied customer requirements (own illustration 2009)**

While doing the problem and request analysis the first task is a high quality stake- and shareholder analysis, to ensure that all affected parties are covered. After that the identified problems and communicated requests can be formulated and brought together.

**As a case example:** The executive management of the SMB defines in its strategy that the business will concentrate on the core business. All additional processes next to value creation processes have to be outsourced or outtasked. This topic influences the:

- **Strategic perspective**. The concerned IT department has possibly changed to a profit centre structure. The department becomes a corporate entity in its own right. Compared with the given situation, additional tasks and processes have to be established like a portfolio management for provided systems or services. To ensure that all future customer requests are well understood, communicated and stated, a demand management has to be implemented or an existing one enhanced.

- The **financial perspective** is also affected. The charging system may have to change from internal accounting to a billing system. The production costs have to be allocated accurately. The fixed costs have to be over-worked to ensure that artificial overhead costs were detected and allocated rightly.

- The provided solutions of the IT department are maybe actually concentrated to the different departments of business. For the case of outsourcing, the IT department becomes a service provider, thus a supplier for the SMB. Therefore the provided solutions have to be clear defined and managed. From the **functionality perspective** it becomes necessary to define manageable units for functional agreements, billing and quality reviews. The former IT department has to define its products: the services.

- As a corporate entity in its own right, the future service provider has to be responsible for service availability and continuity within the **quality perspective**. If the customer experiences a business interruption resulting from a technical failure, the service provider has to be prepared with appropriate protection like SLAs, and contracts with suppliers; Especially in the question of liability.

- When the SMB outsources its IT, it becomes not less important for its business as before. The business wants a sense of security and demands relevant transparency of the further development of core applications and handling of change requests. The **transparency perspective** becomes important if the SMB must have a very short time-to-market for its products.

### 5.3.3 Definition of the nominal state

**The second step** of Thommen's problem solving process for reorganisation (see Figure 29) is to define the objectives for the new form of organisation. Ultimate target of organisational measures and tasks is the most advantageous division of work and responsibilities to increase efficiency and thus the success of the SMB. This target refers to the functional organisation, the process organisation or both. (cf. Thommen 2003, p. 744).

The implementation of ITIL framework as initiation for a reorganisation demands a holistic approach when it is defined. The previous analysis of initial position was overall done and so the setting of the objectives for the reorganisation shall be done just as well. Thommen describes organisational forms in practice. Thereby he draws distinctions inter alia between functional organisation, line and staff organisation, business unit organisation and matrix organisation. (cf. Thommen 2003, p. 792 ff.).

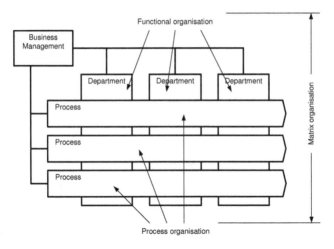

**Figure 31: Schematical diagram of a functional organisation, process organisation and a matrix organisation (own illustration 2009)**

While the different activities of ITIL are covered by processes, skills, know-how, customer interfaces, responsibilities and so on are assigned to units of the functional organisation. Furthermore ITIL also recommends next to the processes functions for enabling Service Management (see chapter 3.4.6 to 3.4.9). All of the peer group members (see chapter 4.4) decided to setup a matrix organisation (see

Figure 31). This kind of organisation ensures best efficiency of engaged resources because technical expertise for example could be concentrated in a software developer unit. There is all expertise, experience and legacy knowledge provided for the different processes in the different service lifecycle stages. If the decision comes for a pure process organisation, these resources have to be established per process and the change of knowledge and experience has to be assured by high effort. Spending awareness on that and continuing the case example from chapter 5.3.2 (outsourcing of all processes next to the value creation processes of an SMB), the organisational structure as well as the process organisation have to be considered.

- From the **strategic perspective**: the concerned IT department, which shall become an outsourced service provider, has to provide its services to the business which concentrates on its core processes. It is recommended to rethink the way how the IT department's outcome has to be organised in order that the business formulates its demands per process or activity. As a nominal state from this perspective a clear **demand management** has to be implemented as well as a **service catalogue management**. As long as the outsourced IT department has only the SMB as customer, a proactive portfolio management for business intelligence and forward-looking placement of economical-adequate services is not necessary.

- From the **financial perspective**: Depending from the defined mission for the new service provider, the expected profit of its business has also to be considered. If the outsourcing comes from a fiscal aspect it could be possible, that the IT department shall become a corporate entity in its own rights but without a view to gain. Similar to a centre concept[16], as it is common practice at large enterprises, the new service provider has to focus at adherence to an agreed budget like a cost centre. This and the new kind of organisation of provider's outcome via services (also cost units) a **financial management** process has to be implemented.

---

[16] Form of business unit organisation: cost centre organisation, profit centre organisation, investment centre organisation (cf. Thommen 2003, p. 795f.)

- From the **functionality perspective:** The most important organisational change is that, providers outcome has to be clear and restrictive agreed and defined. The future service provider has to ensure the functionality of its products and adequate time to market respectively time to customer. Therefore necessary processes are the **service catalogue management, release and deployment management, service asset and configuration management** and **request fulfilment.**

- From the **quality perspective**: To enable service availability, reliability and continuity the technical expertise and maintainability has to be controlled by ITIL processes. It is necessary to avoid failures and interruptions within the systems and processes, define and train reactive measures for the case of discontinuity and handle incidents as fast as possible with workaround solutions. Therefore adequate ITIL processes are **IT Service Continuity Management, Testing, Planning and Support, Event Management** and **Incident Management**. Furthermore the analysis and reporting of agreed quality as well as making sure that in the different service lifecycle stages involved parties deliver and operate in line with agreed quality objectives, the **service level management process** is also necessary.

- From the **transparency perspective**: Different processes should enable demands of customers in respect of transparency. It is important for the business to know that its business data are confidential, complete, accurate and protected stored. The implementation of change requests by business should also be controllable for customers. Product managers from business have tight timeframes for their products and therefore need a controllable service provider as a creditable innovation partner. These are the aims for **information security management** and **change management.**

### 5.3.3.1 Nominal functional organisation

For the definition of the nominal state it is important to have both parts of organisation re- or new defined; the functional organisation as well as the process organisation. Most of the peer group members decided not to change the functional organisation (see chapter 4.5) within the ITIL implementation. For the case of an organisational development approach (see chapter 5.1.2) it necessarily needs not to be changed. As described in Table 13 the evolutionary approach is the basic idea. From this point of view the implementation of ITIL framework (process organisation) points out necessary changes of functional organisation. Involved parties can decide further steps. For the case of a Business Reengineering approach (see chapter 5.1.1) the functional organisation has to be newly-created. An approach for this is described in Figure 32 and points out how the functional organisation gets developed from the overall task.

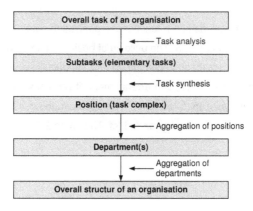

**Figure 32: Creation of a functional organisation approach (own illustration 2009, cf. Thommen 2003, p. 753)**

The first step for the design of functional structure is to divide the overall task of an organisation into subtasks by a task analysis. This has to be done as long as these tasks are not further dispersible or they would get merged while the next step: The task synthesis. During the synthesis, as aforementioned, subtasks get merged to convenient task complexes which are assigned on specific positions. At last all the positions have to be combined to an overall structure in due consideration of all coherences and dependences.

The following three questions have to be considered basically and essentially during the functional organisation design:

- By which criteria has the overall task be divided and separated into elementary tasks?

- By which criteria can elementary tasks be combined and structured to task complexes?

- By which criteria can positions get correlated?

(cf. Thommen 2003, p. 752f.)

The arrangement of positions into a functional organisation could have been done in principle as shown in Figure 33. The building of positions can be done according to accomplishment of tasks or according to the products, services which the service provider is in charge for. The arrangement of positions can also be done by regional conditions as a third feasibility. The subordinate positions can also be accomplishment or object oriented arranged (cf. Thommen 2003, p. 786).

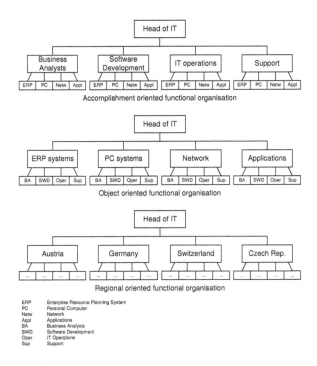

Figure 33: Principles of position arrangements (own illustration 2009, cf. Thommen 2003, p. 787)

## 5.3.3.2 Nominal process organisation

Each organisation can also be seen as a community of people with distinct nuances and interactions. Changing the magnitude of such communities, changes these nuances and interactions dramatically. For this case, different solutions for ITIL process framework implementations are required. Table 16 gives a rough overview about the different characteristics of SMB and large businesses exemplary (cf. Taylor, p. 5f.).

According to the organisation change approach (see chapter 5.1) the way how the implementation of ITIL framework has to be done methodically, has to be designed.

| SMB | Large Business |
|---|---|
| Informal culture | Formal culture |
| Team spirit | Competitiveness |
| Quick communication | Slow communication |
| Responsive | Tendency to inertia |
| Flexible | Constrained |
| Understanding of the business | Isolation from the business |
| Relying on individuals | Broad pool of expertise |
| Nowhere to hide | Role flexibility |
| Wide knowledge | Specialism |
| Limited Knowledge | Comprehensive Knowledge |
| High organisation costs | Economies of scale |
| Per capita complexity | Role division |

**Table 16: Comparison of characteristics of SMB and large businesses**
**(own illustration, cf. Taylor 2007, p. 5f.)**

Contrary to the result of the survey described in chapter 4.5 a Business Reengineering approach is highly recommended for ITIL framework implementation with the aim of Service Management. Why? Most of the peer group members have a Systems Management system before they started to deal with ITIL framework version 2 or 3. But they did not change to Service Management while implementing ITIL framework. In the worst cases members implemented more ITIL processes which are bearably by Systems Management. If an SMB does not request the outcome of the IT department as services in the sense of ITIL, the question is which aim has a service portfolio management or service catalogue management process? For the definition of the nominal state of the process organisation in case of Business Reengineering approach, the question which management system approach the SMB would like to use has to be clarified at first. Based on the conclusion of the peer group members, Table 17 gives an overview of three implementation structure approaches for different system and Service Management purposes. The case example of chapter 5.3.2 is also continued within this table.

| Process/Function | Primary source | Further expansion | Case Example | In-house IT department, cost centre, with legacy systems in the main | Assumption In-house IT department, cost centre, with standard software (partly outtasked) in the main | In-house or outsourced IT department, cost or profit centre, with legacy systems or standard software |
|---|---|---|---|---|---|---|
| Service Management approach | - | - | X | X | - | X |
| Systems Management approach | - | - | - | X | X | - |
| Demand management | SS | SD | X | - | - | 1. WP |
| Financial management | SS | - | X | - | - | 1. WP |
| Service Portfolio management | SS | SD | - | - | - | - |
| Service strategy | SS | - | - | - | - | - |
| Availability management | SD | CSI | - | 3. WP | 4. WP | 3. WP |
| Capacity management | SD | SO, CSI | - | - | 4. WP | 3. WP |
| Information Security management | SD | SO, CSI | X | ongoing | ongoing | ongoing |
| IT Service Continuity management | SD | CSI | X | 3. WP | 4. WP | 3. WP |
| Service Catalogue management | SD | SS | X | - | - | 1. WP |
| Service Level management | SD | CSI | X | - | 3. WP | 4. WP |
| Supplier management | SD | - | - | - | 3. WP | 4. WP |
| Change management | ST | - | X | 2. WP | 2. WP | 2. WP |
| Evaluation | ST | - | - | - | - | - |
| Knowledge management | ST | CSI | - | - | - | 5. WP |
| Release and deployment management | ST | SO, CSI | X | 2. WP | 2. WP | 2. WP |
| Service Asset and configuration management | ST | SO, CSI | X | 2. WP | 2. WP | 2. WP |
| Service validation and testing | ST | - | - | - | - | 2. WP |
| Testing planning and support | ST | - | X | 2. WP | 2. WP | 2. WP |
| Access management | SO | - | - | - | - | - |
| Application management | SO | - | - | - | - | - |
| Event management | SO | CSI | X | - | - | 5. WP |
| Incident management | SO | CSI | X | 1. WP | 1. WP | 5. WP |
| IT Operations management | SO | - | - | - | - | - |
| Problem management | SO | CSI | - | - | 1. WP | 5. WP |
| Request fulfilment | SO | - | X | - | 1. WP | 5. WP |
| Service desk | SO | - | - | - | - | - |
| Technical management | SO | - | - | - | - | - |
| 7-step improvement process | CSI | - | - | - | - | 1. WP |
| Service measurement | CSI | - | - | - | 3. WP | 4. WP |
| Service reporting | CSI | - | - | - | 3. WP | 4. WP |

**Table 17: Approach for an ITIL framework implementation structure (own illustration 2009)**

Implementation of the ITIL framework within an SMB is recommended to be done to some extent and in groups. A defined SMB which attended the peer group in chapter 4.3 has about 21,9 staff members (FTE) dealing with IT topics on average. All decided ITIL processes and functions have to be covered by these people next to their operational responsibilities. This limited number of human resources requires an efficient and on the essentials concentrated combination of ITIL framework recommendations. The ITIL processes as described in chapter 3 are a best practice management system solution, adaptable for all kinds and sizes of IT service providers. So it is fundamental necessary not to implement everything blindly but rather adapted. Table 17 shows such adoptions which combine recommended processes to work packages (WP) and avoid processes which are oversized, generate more effort as benefit comes out or have no appreciation of the decided management system (see Figure 1) or centre organisation (see footnote 16). The major influences on how these work packages are combined include following points:

- Staff attitudes, making possible overlap, cross-function working and correlative support between ITIL processes.

- Restrictions on ITIL process scopes, both because of staff, skill and financial limitations, and because the complexity and rigour appropriate for mainstream ITIL processes are not that necessary.

- Experiences of the peer group members with ITIL framework implementation as described in chapter 4.5Requirements and non-requirements in principle according to decided cost centre and management system.

There are also aspects for the definition of nominal process organisation which are relevant for all sizes of organisation but which are better visible in a small scale, where they are also easier to deal with. These are for example staff member education and awareness, where a more flexible approach can be taken when dealing with smaller numbers (cf. Taylor 2007, p.43). The numbering gives a hint for the sequence of implementation.

## 5.3.4 Setup of an organisational change project

The efficient holistic implementation plan of the ITIL framework for SMBs in due consideration of all coherences and dependences as described before, demands project management methods to become efficient through planning and implementation phase. Step one and two of the problem solving process for reorganisation[17] (see Figure 29) ensures that all coherences and dependences are identified, described and correlated. Step three assures the efficiency of implementation by description which project management methods should be used in which context.

### 5.3.4.1 Project Management standards and recommendations

Different organisations for Project Management methods compete against each other for the attention of potential customers. The most notable are:

- International Project Management Association (IPMA) with the pm-baseline appropriate for each current country.

- Project Management Institute (PMI) with the Guide to the Project Management body of knowledge (PMBOK Guide).

- OGC with the Projects in Controlled Environments (PRINCE2).

The fourth edition of the PMBOK is valid at present and also used as an ANSI-standard for Project Management. This makes it very useful for businesses whose value creation is done by projects. These businesses can certify their staff members as PMI-project managers which increase their chances by call for tenders. The PMBOK consists of five project management process groups and nine knowledge areas which bring out 42 advices for methods (cf. PMI 2008, p. 43).

---

[17] Step one and two are described within chapters 5.3.1 to 5.3.3. Step three is described within chapter 5.3.4.

The PRINCE2 project management standard was released in June 2009 as a refreshed version of the initial one published in 2005. It is a process oriented approach of project management which makes it very useful for organisations who deal with a high number of projects in their daily business. PRINCE2 describes seven themes, seven processes with 40 activities, eight roles and process based checklists (cf. Best Management Practice 2009c, Best Management Practice 2009d).

The IPMA is an international association of national project management institutes. As distinguished from the PMI and OGC, IPMA does not provide worldwide valid standard methods for project management. The matter of IPMA is a common definition of requirements on people who want to become certified project managers. This certification model knows four stages of education for project management assistance to project management executives. Each national project management institute provides its own baseline with national standard methods and recommendations for project management in due consideration of the international valid IPMA Competence Baseline (ICB). The national institutes in Austria, Germany and Switzerland are:

- In Austria Projekt Management Austria (www.p-m-a.at)

- In Germany GPM Deutsche Gesellschaft für Projektmanagement E.V. (www.gpm-ipma.de)

- In Switzerland Swiss Project Management Association (www.spm.ch)

(cf. IPMA 2006, 1ff.)

For the following setup of project management methods for an efficient holistic ITIL framework implementation in due consideration of all coherences and dependencies, the recommendations and templates of above listed project management organisations and institutes are used cross benched and consolidated.

## 5.3.4.2 Project management methods for use

Based on the above listed approach, the environment analysis, the problem and known unsatisfied customer requirements analysis, the definition of nominal state and implementation plan have to be covered by project management methods. A matching with project management methods is listed in Table 18.

| Holistic implementation plan approach | Project management method |
|---|---|
| Project Management | • Project organisation |
| Stake- and shareholder analysis<br>• Identification of the project environment<br>• Structuring of influencing values<br>• Validation of the environment and a detailed analysis<br>• Derivation of measures | • Environment analysis |
| Analysis of known problems and unsatisfied customer requirements<br>• Strategic perspective<br>• Financial perspective<br>• Functionality perspective<br>• Quality perspective<br>• Transparency perspective | • Cause and effect diagram |
| Definition of nominal state<br>• Nominal functional organisation<br>• Nominal process organisation<br>• Cost Benefit Analysis<br>• Total Cost of Ownership | • Object breakdown structure |
| Implementation plan<br>• For Business Reengineering approach<br>• For organisational development approach | • Work breakdown structure<br>• Bar chart |

**Table 18: Matching holistic implementation plan with project management methods (own illustration 2009)**

During planning and creation of project management documents, the interdependencies between the project management methods have to be taken into account as illustrated in Figure 34. Dashed lined methods are not in scope of implementation plan because they depend on own standards and methods of specific SMBs which decide to implement ITIL framework.

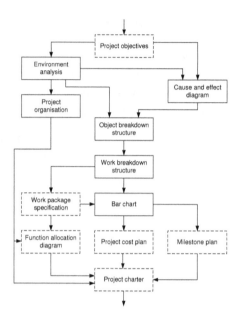

**Figure 34: Relationship between project management methods during
project setup process (own illustration 2009)**

## 5.3.4.3 Environment analysis

This project management method is described in more detail in Patzak et al 2009,
chapter 2.1.5, p. 94ff. Further description of the environment analysis procedure is
given in chapter 5.3.1.

Aim: Holistic and in time identification of all influencing values on the IT
department or service provider. Furthermore the identification of dependencies
and coherences to other projects, stake- and shareholders.

Procedure: Identification of the project environment, structuring of influencing
values (see Appendix B), validation of the environment and a detailed analysis
(see Appendix C) and derivation of measures.

### 5.3.4.4 Project organisation

Aim: Temporary organisation of the SMBs ITIL implementation project to ensure efficient and direct communication as well as best possible clear and articulately formulation of project objectives, tasks and results. IT is important to assign project roles with concerned persons. The way how the IT department provides its services affects the whole SMB. Therefore the sponsor of the projects shall be the SMB executive anyway.

Procedure: Setup of organisation (see Appendix D) and Setup of meeting cycles and responsibilities.

### 5.3.4.5 Cause and effect diagram

Aim: To ensure that all conditions for an ITIL framework implementation are covered. A structured approach to detect the root cause of known problems and unsatisfied customer requirements is basically liable for the awareness of actually needed measures and solutions (see chapter 5.3.2).

Procedure: Definition of adequate perspectives for analysis, definition of basic questions and treatment of known problems and unsatisfied customer requirements in consideration of basic questions (see Appendix E).

### 5.3.4.6 Object breakdown structure (OBS)

Aim: Definition of all objects which get delivered or changed during the ITIL framework implementation to ensure all deliverables as well as dependencies and coherences are identified and get addressed while implementation.

Procedure: Derivation of necessary new or changed processes and functional units of the cause and effect diagram (see Appendix F).

### 5.3.4.7 Work breakdown structure (WBS)

Aim: The work breakdown structure contains all tasks which have to be performed in an ITIL framework implementation project, structured in phases topically. With the work breakdown structure project tasks get scaled into work packages which are the planning basis for responsibilities, start and end dates, costs etc.

Procedure: Going through the OBS and defining which tasks are necessary to fulfil the deliverables, structuring of these tasks into work packages and phases and if applicable, assignment of responsibilities, budget and duration times (with start and end date) to work packages (see Appendix G).

### 5.3.4.8 Bar chart

Aim: The phases and work packages as defined in the WBS, become illustrated in a bar chart plan to demonstrate the dependencies, antecessor and successor as well as to visualise duration, start and end dates.

Procedure: Going through the WBS and identification of dependencies between the phases and work packages and illustration in bar chart form with links between the work packages and mile stones (see Appendix H).

# 6 Conclusion

ITIL framework is overarching and not a technical issue. ITIL framework provides processes, roles, methods and techniques for IT providers to become service providers. The decision of technicians or available quality managers to implement operational parts of ITIL in order to see whether it can be an additional benefit or saving of costs often comes along with a source of errors. This is not only my personal conclusion; a lot of people who deal with ITIL for years in their professional environment agree on it. Major mistakes during ITIL framework implementations are in extracts:

- There is no vision for application of ITIL. No one is sure of what is happening with ITIL and there are no clear answers.

- Top-down commitment of executive management is not necessary. The project can be infiltrated via middle management.

- ITIL is not a strategic project, thus existing resources to implement it can be used.

(cf. SearchCIO.com, 2009)

ITIL framework does not provide any technological solutions and fixes. It provides rather a holistic management system for business development and quality improvement of provided IT. The functionality of an engaged application will not be affected. A conclusion of this master thesis is the formidable cognition that the major approach for an implementation is nothing else than a normal organisational change for process implementation or improvement with all impacts on existing functional and process organisations. Therefore necessary goals have to be evaluated and set as first move, just as for a normal organisation change project.

One of the real benefits of ITIL framework is the origination of transparency of costs and performance of staff members and systems. Inferentially the beneficiary is superficial the customer and further the head of IT departments or providers, because measurable data can be agreed and controlled seriously. An organisational change, what ITIL triggers, affects more or less existing claims of middle management and devaluate their unique selling propositions (USP). Therefrom a strong gruelling resistance of the middle management will emerge in all probability and annoys all endeavours as long as it will not work successfully. Because of that, a top down commitment and approach is a fundamental success factor to generate benefits of an ITIL implementation.

A major conclusion of this master thesis is that costs saving characteristics of ITIL framework do not appear by ITIL framework implementation. They appear in case of consistent application. For that reason, half-assed implementation without a plan generates ineffectual benefits out of it.

ITIL will not succeed if it is done for the sake of ITIL and if it is done as something secondary. Also the substitutional character of implementing new has to be accommodated. If an organisation has already legacy processes in place and the decision is made for change to ITIL, the existing processes must be unhanded such an adequate process is newly implemented. The change from Systems Management (operation and projects) to Service Management is not done solidly in the majority of cases.

# 7 List of figures

# 8 List of tables

# 9 List of abbreviations

| | |
|---|---|
| 20000 | ISO/IEC 20000-1:2005 – Information Technology – Service Management, Part 1: Specification |
| AMIS | Availability Management Information System |
| ANSI | American National Standards Intitute |
| Appl | Application |
| ASP | Application Service Provision |
| AST | Agreed Service Time |
| BA | Business Analysis |
| BIA | Business Impact Analysis |
| BPO | Business Process Outsourcing |
| BSM | Business Service Management |
| CAB | Change Advisory Board |
| CFIA | Component Failure Impact Analysis |
| CI(s) | Configuration Item(s) |
| CIP | Continuous improvement process |
| CMDB | Configuration Management Database |
| CMIS | Capacity Management Information System |
| CMMI | Capability Maturity Model Integration |
| CMS | Configuration Management System |

| | |
|---|---|
| CSF | Critical Success Factor |
| CSI | Continual Service Improvement |
| CSP | Core Service Package |
| DIKW | Data-Information-Knowledge-Wisdom |
| DML | Definitive Media Library |
| ECAB | Emergency Change Advisory Board |
| EFQM | European Foundation for Quality Management |
| ELS | Early Life Support |
| ERP | Enterprise Resource Planning System |
| EU | European Union |
| FTA | Fault Tree Analysis |
| FTE | Full time equivalent |
| GITMM | Government Information Technology Infrastructure Management Methodology |
| HM Treasury | Her Majesty's Treasury |
| HR | Human Resources |
| ICB | IPMA Competence Baseline |
| IPMA | International Project Management Association |
| ISMS | Information Security Management System |
| ISO | International Organization for Standardization |
| IT | Information Technology |

| | |
|---|---|
| ITIL | Information Technology Infrastructure Library |
| ITSCM | IT Service Contiunity Management |
| ITSM | Information Technology Service Management |
| itSMF | Information Technology Service Management Forum |
| itSMFI | Information Technology Service Management Forum International |
| KEDB | Known Error Database |
| KPI | Key Performance Indicator |
| KPO | Knowledge Process Outsourcing |
| KVP | Kontinuierlicher Verbesserungsprozess |
| LOS | Line of Service |
| Mgmt | Management |
| MTBF | Mean time between failures |
| MTBSI | Mean time between system incidents |
| MTRS | Mean time to restore service |
| NACE | Nomenclature statistique des activités économiques dans la Communauté européenne |
| Netw | Network |
| OBS | Object breakdown structure |
| OGC | Office of Government Commerce |
| OLA | Operational Level Agreement |

| ÖNACE | Österreich Nomenclature statistique des activités économiques dans la Communauté européenne |
| --- | --- |
| Oper | IT Operations |
| PC | Personal Computer |
| PIR | Post Implementation Review |
| PMBOK | A Guide to the Project Management body of knowledge |
| PMI | Project Management Institute |
| PSA | Projected Service Availability |
| RfC(s) | Request for Change(s) |
| ROI | Return on Investment |
| ROIC | Return on Invested Capital |
| SACM | Service Asset and Configuration Management |
| SCD | Supplier Contract Database |
| SCM | Service Catalogue Management |
| SD | Service Design |
| SDP | Service Design Package |
| SEI | Software Engineering Institute |
| SFA | Service Failure Analysis |
| SIP | Service Improvement Plan |
| SKMS | Service Knowledge Management System |
| SLA | Service Level Agreement |

# 9 List of abbreviations

| | |
|---|---|
| SLM | Service Level Management |
| SLP | Service Level Package |
| SLR | Service Level Requirement |
| SMB | Small and medium-sized business |
| SO | Service Operation |
| SPM | Service Portfolio Management |
| SPO | Service provisioning organisation |
| SPOC | Single point of contact |
| SPOF | Single Point of Failure |
| SS | Service Strategy |
| ST | Service Transition |
| Sup | Support |
| SWD | Software Development |
| UC | Underpinning Contract |
| USP | Unique selling proposition |
| VCD | Variable Cost Dynamics |
| WBS | Work breakdown structure |
| WKO | Wirtschaftskammer Österreich |
| WP | Work package |

# 10 Bibliography

Books

**Cartlidge, Alison; Hanna, Ashley; Rudd, Colin; Macfarlane, Ivor; Windebank, John; Rance, Stuart:** An Introductory Overview of ITIL V3, A high-level overview of the IT Infrastructure Library, version 1.0. IT Service Management Forum Limited, United Kingdom, 2007

**Gareis, Roland:** Happy Projects, 3. Auflage. Manz, Wien, 2006

**Hammer, Michael; Champy, James:** Business Reenginieering. Die Radikalkur für das Unternehmen, 3. Auflage. Campus Verlag, Frankfurt am Main, 1994

**International Organization for Standardization (ISO):** ISO/IEC 20000-1:2005 – Information Technology – Service Management, Part 1: Specification, first edition, Dec., 15th. 2005. ISO/IEC, Geneva, 2005a

**International Organization for Standardization (ISO):** ISO/IEC 20000-1:2005 – Information Technology – Service Management, Part 2: Code of Practice, first edition, Dec., 15th 2005. ISO/IEC, Geneva, 2005b

**International Project Management Association (IPMA):** ICB - IPMA Competence Baseline, Version 3.0. International Project Management Association, Nijerk, 2006

**Kiechl, Rolf: Management of Change. In Thommen, Jean Paul (Issuer):** Management Kompetenz. Versus, Zürich, 1995

**Office of Government Commerce (OGC):** Continual Service Improvement, 09/07, second impression with corrections 2007. The Stationary Office (TSO), Norwich, 2007a

**Office of Government Commerce (OGC):** ITIL® V3 Foundation Handbook, 11/08. The Stationary Office (TSO), Norwich, 2008

**Office of Government Commerce (OGC):** *Service Design*, second impression with corrections 2007. The Stationary Office (TSO), Norwich, 2007b

**Office of Government Commerce (OGC):** *Service Operation*, 09/07, second impression 2007. The Stationary Office (TSO), Norwich, 2007c

**Office of Government Commerce (OGC):** *Service Strategy*, 09/07, second impression with corrections 2007. The Stationary Office (TSO), Norwich, 2007d

**Office of Government Commerce (OGC):** *Service Transition*, 09/07, second impression with corrections 2007. The Stationary Office (TSO), Norwich, 2007e

**Office of Government Commerce (OGC):** *The Official Introduction to the ITIL Service Lifecycle*, 08/07. The Stationary Office (TSO), Norwich, 2007f

**Patzak, Gerold; Rattay, Günter:** *Projektmanagement, Leitfaden zum Management von Projekten, Projektportfolios, Programmen und projektorientierten Unternehmen*, 5. Auflage. Linde Verlag, Wien, 2009

**Project Management Institute (PMI):** *A Guide to the project management body of knowledge (PMBOK® GUIDE), Fourth Edition*. Project Management Institute Inc., Pennsylvania, 2008

**Schanz, Günther:** *Organisationsgestaltung. Struktur und Verhalten*. Vahlen, München, 1982

**Stockmann, Reinhard:** *Evaluation und Qualitätsentwicklung. Eine Grundlage für wirkungsorientiertes Qualitätsmanagement*, Band 5. Waxmann Verlag, Münster, 2006

**Taylor, Sharon; Macfarlane, Ivor:** *ITIL® Small-scale Implementation*, Third Impression. The Stationary Office (TSO), Norwich, 2007

**Thommen, Jean-Paul; Achleitner, Ann-Kristin:** *Allgemeine Betriebswirtschaftslehre*, 4., überarbeitete und erweiterte Auflage.

Betriebswirtschaftlicher Verlag Dr. Th. Gabler/GWV Fachverlage GmbH, Wiesbaden, 2003

**Van Bon, Jan; de Jong, Arjen; Kolthof, Axel; Pieper, Mike; Tjassing, Ruby; van der Veen, Annelies; Verheijen, Tieneke:** *Foundations of IT Service Management Based on ITIL V3*, third edition, first impression. Van Haren Publishing, Zaltbommel, 2007

**Van Bon, Jan; de Jong, Arjen; Kolthof, Axel; Pieper, Mike; Tjassing, Ruby; van der Veen, Annelies; Verheijen, Tieneke:** *IT Service Management Based on ITIL® V3; A Pocket Guide*, first edition, third impression. Van Haren Publishing, Zaltbommel, 2008

# 10 Bibliography

Websites

**Best Management Practice:** ITIL V3 Acronyms v1.0, 30 May 2007
URL: http://www.best-management-practice.com/gempdf/
ITILV3_Acronyms_English_v1_2007.pdf (April, 18th 2009a)

**Best Management Practice:** ITIL V3 Glossary, v01, 30 May 2007
URL: http://www.best-management-practice.com/gempdf/
ITILV3_Glossary_English_v1_2007.pdf (April, 18th 2009b)

**Best Management Practice:** Ogc's Best Practice Users: Case studies and testimonials
URL: http://www.best-management-practice.com/Knowledge-Centre/OGCs-Best-Practice-Users-Case-Studies-and-Testimonials (August, 5th 2009c)

**Best Management Practice:** PRINCE2 2009 Overview Brochure
URL: http://www.best-management-practice.com/gempdf/
PRINCE2_2009_Overview_Brochure_June2009.pdf (August, 5th 2009d)

**International Organization for Standardization (ISO):** About ISO
URL: http://www.iso.org/iso/about.htm (April, 18th 2009)

**Office of Government Commerce (OGC):** About us
URL: http://www.ogc.gov.uk/about_ogc_who_we_are.asp (April, 18th 2009)

**PROJEKT MANAGEMENT AUSTRIA:** pm baseline v 3.0, englisch
URL: http://debian.p-m-a.at/download/download%202009/
pm%20baseline%203%200.pdf (August, 5th 2009)

**Projektmagazin:** Glossar
URL: http://www.projektmagazin.de/glossar/gl-0846.html (July, 25th 2009)

**SearchCIO.com:** 10 ITIL implementation mistakes and fixes
URL: http://searchcio.techtarget.com/news/article/0,289142,sid182_gci1304
412,00.html (August, 17th 2009)

**Software Engineering Institute (SEI):** About the SEI

URL: http://www.sei.cmu.edu/about (July, 25th 2009a)

**Software Engineering Institute (SEI):** What is CMMI?

URL: http://www.sei.cmu.edu/cmmi/general/index.html (July, 25th 2009b)

**Statistik Austria:** Klassifikationsdatenbank, ÖNACE 2008 – Struktur

URL: http://www.statistik.at/KDBWeb/kdb_VersionAuswahl.do (August, 15th 2009)

10 Bibliography

Miscellaneous

**Amtsblatt der Europäischen Union,** *Empfehlung der Kommission vom 6. Mai 2003 betreffend die Definition der Kleinstunternehmen sowie der kleinen und mittleren Unternehmen* (Bekannt gegeben unter Aktenzeichen K(2003) 1422), (2003/361/EG), L124/36 herausgegeben am 20.5.2003

**HEROLD Business Data GmbH:** *Herold Marketing CD business*, status January 2001

# Appendix A

**Questionnaire**

An

Geschäftsführung eines KMU

Sehr geehrte Damen und Herren,

mein Name ist Jochen Höfenstock. Ich studiere seit 2004 berufsbegleitend an der Fachhochschule des bfi Wien (Diplomstudiengang Projektmanagement und Informationstechnik). Im Zuge des Studiums verfasse ich eine Diplomarbeit mit dem Titel *„An efficient holistic implementation plan of the ITIL framework version 3 for small an medium-sized business (SMB) in due consideration of all coherences and dependences to assure optimum quality of implementation."*

Um dabei auf die Bedürfnisse und Anforderungen von kleinen und mittelständischen Unternehmen aufsetzen zu können, bitte ich Sie um Ihre Unterstützung. Füllen Sie bitte beigefügten Fragenkatalog bis **28. Februar 2009** aus und schicken Sie ihn am Postweg oder elektronisch an:

> Postanschrift       Email
> Jochen Höfenstock


> 1070 Wien, Österreich

Alle Ihre Angaben werden selbstverständlich anonymisiert statistisch aufbereitet und in der Diplomarbeit berücksichtigt. Die fertige Diplomarbeit wird für fünf Jahre gesperrt. Als Dank für Ihre Unterstützung lasse ich Ihnen gerne ein Exemplar der fertigen Diplomarbeit sowie der erhobenen, anonymisierten Daten zukommen. Füllen Sie bitte dafür das letzte Blatt des Fragebogens aus. Selbstverständlich werden der ausgefüllte Fragebogen und das letzte Blatt nach Einlangen umgehend getrennt voneinander abgelegt um so Diskretion und Anonymität sicherstellen zu können.

Appendix

Ich möchte mich vorweg recht herzlich für Ihre Unterstützung und Mitarbeit bedanken, nur mit einer hohen Menge an Daten erhält diese Umfrage einen breiten, repräsentativen Aussagewert. **Machen sie bitte mit!**

Vielen Dank für Ihre Unterstützung,

Jochen Höfenstock

| Nr. | Frage |
|---|---|
| 1 | Fragen zum Unternehmen |
| 1.a | Wie viele Mitarbeiter (FTE ... Full Time Equivalent) beschäftigt Ihr Unternehmen (Zur Einstufung des Fragebogens als KMU-Unternehmen gemäß Amtsblatt der Europäischen Union K(2003) 1422)?<br><br>*Angaben bei FTE auch mit Kommawerten möglich (zB. 15,4)* |
| 1.b | Wie viele Mitarbeiter (FTE) davon beschäftigen Sie ausschließlich im IT-Bereich (Administratoren, Techniker, Software Entwickler, IT-Projektleiter)? Bitte berücksichtigen Sie nur unternehmensintern angestellte Mitarbeiter.<br><br>*Angaben bei FTE auch mit Kommawerten möglich (zB. 15,4)* |
| 1.c | Wie viele Mitarbeiter (FTE) davon beschäftigen Sie ausschließlich im IT-Bereich ohne feste Anstellung (Werkvertrag, Time and material based, externe Leistungspartner etc.)?<br><br>*Angaben bei FTE auch mit Kommawerten möglich (zB. 15,4)* |
| 1.d | Wie hoch ist der Jahresumsatz Ihres Unternehmens (in Mio. Euro) (Zur Einstufung des Fragebogens als KMU-Unternehmen gemäß Amtsblatt der Europäischen Union K(2003) 1422)? |
| 1.e | Wie hoch belaufen sich die IT-Kosten Ihres Unternehmens per Jahr relativ zu den Gesamtkosten des Unternehmens (in Prozent)? |
| 1.f | Die IT-Dienste zur Unterstützung der Unternehmensgeschäftsprozesse können grundlegend in Betriebsaktivitäten und Innovationsaktivitäten unterschieden werden. Betriebsaktivitäten sind alle Aufwände, welche bestehende IT-Dienste betreiben und kontinuierliche verbessern (IT-Operation). Innovationsaktivitäten sind alle Aufwände, welche bestehende IT-Dienste grundlegend verändern, verbessern bzw. außer Dienst stellen oder neue IT-Dienste basierend auf den internen Kundenanforderungen einführen (IT-Projekte). Führen Sie bitte an, in welchem Verhältnis Ihre jährlichen Unternehmens IT-Kosten aufgeteilt werden. |

| Jährliche IT-Kosten (in Prozent) | Antwort |
|---|---|
| | Betriebsaktivitäten |
| | Innovationsaktivitäten |

*Die Summe ergibt 100%*

| 1.g | Wie viele Mitarbeiter (FTE) ihrer internen IT-Abteilung oder von externen Leistungspartner beschäftigen Sie in folgenden Funktionen? |
|---|---|

| Anzahl FTEs unternehmens-intern | Anzahl FTEs externer Leistungspartner | Antwort |
|---|---|---|
| | | Management (Bereichsleitung, Abteilungsleitung, Prozess- und/oder Projektmanagement etc.) |
| | | Business Analysis (fachliche Kundenschnittstelle, Demand Management, Abstimmung und Spezifikation der Anforderungen etc.) |
| | | Software Development (Softwareentwicklung, Testing und Engineering) |
| | | Infrastruktur und Betrieb (Netzwerktechnologie, Server- und Softwarebetrieb, Service bzw. Help Desk) |

*Angaben bei FTE auch mit Kommawerten möglich (zB. 15,4)*

| 1.h | Nach welchem Wirtschaftszweig ist Ihr Unternehmen klassifiziert (Klassifizierung gemäß ÖNACE 2008)? |
|---|---|

*Weiterführende Informationen zur Klassifizierung nach ÖNACE erhalten Sie unter http://www.statistik.at/KDBWeb//pages/Kdb_versionDetail.jsp?#4074225*

| 2 | Fragen zur Organisation Ihres Unternehmens |
|---|---|

| 2.a | Ist die Aufbauorganisation Ihres Unternehmens bekannt und dokumentiert? |
|---|---|

| X | Antwort |
|---|---|
| | Ja, aber nicht dokumentiert. |
| | Ja, auf Organigramm beschrieben. |
| | Ja, auf Organigramm beschrieben. Die Dokumentation ist allerdings meist nicht aktuell. |

*X ... Bitte entsprechende Aussage markieren*

| 2.b | Ist die Ablauforgansiation Ihres Unternehmens bekannt und dokumentiert? |
|---|---|

| X | Antwort |
|---|---|
| | Ja, aber nicht dokumentiert. |
| | Ja, auf Prozesslandkarte beschrieben. |
| | Ja, auf Prozesslandkarte beschrieben. Die Dokumentation ist allerdings meist nicht aktuell. |

Appendix

| X ... *Bitte entsprechende Aussage markieren* | |
|---|---|
| 2.c | **Welche Reifegradaussage trifft auf die Geschäftsprozesse Ihres Unternehmens zu?** |

| X | Antwort |
|---|---|
| | 1 – Initial<br>Prozesse sind nicht definiert. Zeitpläne, Lieferergebnisse und Kosten sind nicht vorhersagbar und meßbar. |
| | 2 – Managed<br>Prozesse sind erkannt und werden geführt (managed). Ähnliche Prozesse sind wiederholbar. |
| | 3 – Defined<br>Prozesse sind erkannt und dokumentiert. Prozessrollen sind erkannt und dokumentiert. Ein organisationsweiter KVP ist etabliert. |
| | 4 – Quantitatively Managed<br>Reifegrad „Defined" und es wird eine nachweisliche statistische Prozesskontrolle durchgeführt. |
| | 5 – Optimizing<br>Reifegrad „Quantitavely Managed" und die Prozesse werden anhand der statistischen Prozesskontrolle nachweislich verbessert. |

*X ... Bitte entsprechende Aussage markieren*

| 2.d | Welche Organisationsform trifft auf Ihr Unternehmen zu? |
|---|---|

| X | Antwort |
|---|---|
| | Nur Aufbauorganisation ist definiert |
| | Nur Ablauforganisation ist definiert |
| | Eine Matrixorganisation ist definiert |

*X ... Bitte entsprechende Aussage markieren*

| 3 | Fragen zur Anwendung von ITIL in Version 3 in Ihrem Unternehmen und damit einhergehenden Organisationsänderungen. |
|---|---|
| 3.a | Welchen Organisationsänderungsansatz wählten Sie zur vollständigen oder teilweisen Einführung von ITIL Version 3 in Ihrem Unternehmen? |

| X | Antwort |
|---|---|
| | Business Reengineeringansatz |
| | Organisationsentwicklungsansatz |

*X ... Bitte entsprechende Aussage markieren*

| 3.b | Haben Sie im Zuge der vollständigen oder teilweisen Einführung von ITIL Version 3 in Ihr Unternehmen die bestehende Aufbauorganisation geändert? |
|---|---|

| X | Antwort |
|---|---|
| | Ja |
| | Nein |

*X ... Bitte entsprechende Aussage markieren*

| 3.c | Welche Methode haben Sie bei der vollständigen oder teilweisen Einführung |
|---|---|

| von ITIL Version 3 in Ihrem Unternehmen gewählt? |
|---|

| X | Antwort |
|---|---|
| | Kontinuierlicher Verbesserungsprozess (KVP) |
| | Capability Maturity Model Integration (CMMI) |
| | Evaluation |

*X ... Bitte entsprechende Aussage markieren*

**3.d** Welche Grundeigenschaft der Unternehmens-internen IT-Dienstleistungen wollten Sie mit der vollständigen oder teilweisen Einführung von ITIL Version 3 in Ihr Unternehmen verbessern? Bitte markieren Sie nur eine!

| X | Antwort |
|---|---|
| | Finanzwesen, Kosten |
| | Funktionalität |
| | Qualität |
| | Transparenz der Betriebs- und Projektleistungen |

*X ... Bitte entsprechende Aussage markieren*

**3.e** Würden Sie basierend auf Ihrem Wissen und Ihrer Erfahrung eine vollständige Einführung von ITIL Version 2 oder 3 heute gesamtheitlich angehen, welche Prozesse würden Sie einführen? Beachten Sie bitte das dafür skizzierte Szenario. Kombinieren Sie bitte die ITIL Prozesse und Funktionen sinngemäß zu Arbeitspaketen für deren Einführung.

**Szenario: Unternehmens-interne IT-Abteilung als Cost Center mit hauptsächlich eigenentwickelten Systemen im Betrieb.**

| ITIL framework in version 3 | Process or function in version 3 | Process or function in version 2 | ITIL framework in version 2 | Hier bitte Arbeitspaket-nummerierung eintragen |
|---|---|---|---|---|
| Service Strategy | Demand Management | Capacity Management | Service Delivery | |
| Service Strategy | Financial Management | Financial Management for IT-Services | Service Delivery | |
| Service Strategy | Service Portfolio Management | - | Business Perspective | |
| Service Strategy | Strategy Generation | - | Business Perspective | |
| Service Design | Availability Management | Availability Management | Service Delivery | |
| Service Design | Capacity Management | Capacity Management | Service Delivery | |
| Service Design | Information Security Management | Security Management | Security Management | |
| Service Design | IT Service Continuity Management | IT Service Continuity Management | Service Delivery | |
| Service Design | Service Catalogue Management | Service Level Management | Service Delivery | |
| Service Design | Service Level Management | Service Level Management | Service Delivery | |
| Service Design | Supplier Management | - | Service Delivery | |

| | | | | |
|---|---|---|---|---|
| Service Transition | Change Management | Change Management | Service Support | |
| Service Transition | Evaluation | - | Service Support | |
| Service Transition | Knowledge Management | - | Service Support | |
| Service Transition | Release and Deployment Management | Release Management, Deployment Management | Service Support, ICT Infrastructure Management | |
| Service Transition | Service Asset and Configuration Management | Configuration Management | Service Support | |
| Service Transition | Service Validation and Testing | - | Service Support | |
| Service Transition | Testing Planning and Support | - | Service Support | |
| Service Operation | Access Management | - | Security Management | |
| Service Operation | Event Management | Incident Management | ICT Infrastructure Management | |
| Service Operation | Funktion: Application Management | Application Management | Application Management | |
| Service Operation | Funktion: IT Operations Management | Operations | ICT Infrastructure Management | |
| Service Operation | Funktion: Service Desk | Funktion: Service Desk | Service Support | |
| Service Operation | Funktion: Technical Management | Technical Support | ICT Infrastructure Management | |
| Service Operation | Incident Management | Incident Management | Service Support | |
| Service Operation | Problem Management | Problem Management | Service Support | |
| Service Operation | Request Fulfillment | Incident Management | Service Support | |
| Continual Service Improvement | Business Questions for CSI | - | - | |
| Continual Service Improvement | Service Measurement | - | - | |
| Continual Service Improvement | Return on Investment for CSI | - | - | |
| Continual Service Improvement | Service Reporting | Teil des Service Level Management | Service Delivery | |
| Continual Service Improvement | The 7-Step Improvement Process | - | - | |

3.f Würden Sie basierend auf Ihrem Wissen und Ihrer Erfahrung eine vollständige Einführung von ITIL Version 2 oder 3 heute gesamtheitlich angehen, welche Prozesse würden Sie einführen? Beachten Sie bitte das dafür skizzierte Szenario. Kombinieren Sie bitte die ITIL Prozesse und Funktionen sinngemäß zu Arbeitspaketen für deren Einführung.

**Szenario: Unternehmens-interne IT-Abteilung als Cost Center mit hauptsächlich Standardsystemen (Out-of-the-box, best-of-breed) im Betrieb mit teilweise outtasked Aufgaben.**

Appendix

| ITIL framework in version 3 | Process or function in version 3 | Process or function in version 2 | ITIL framework in version 2 | Hier bitte Arbeitspaket-nummerierung eintragen |
|---|---|---|---|---|
| Service Strategy | Demand Management | Capacity Management | Service Delivery | |
| Service Strategy | Financial Management | Financial Management for IT-Services | Service Delivery | |
| Service Strategy | Service Portfolio Management | - | Business Perspective | |
| Service Strategy | Strategy Generation | - | Business Perspective | |
| Service Design | Availability Management | Availability Management | Service Delivery | |
| Service Design | Capacity Management | Capacity Management | Service Delivery | |
| Service Design | Information Security Management | Security Management | Security Management | |
| Service Design | IT Service Continuity Management | IT Service Continuity Management | Service Delivery | |
| Service Design | Service Catalogue Management | Service Level Management | Service Delivery | |
| Service Design | Service Level Management | Service Level Management | Service Delivery | |
| Service Design | Supplier Management | - | Service Delivery | |
| Service Transition | Change Management | Change Management | Service Support | |
| Service Transition | Evaluation | - | Service Support | |
| Service Transition | Knowledge Management | - | Service Support | |
| Service Transition | Release and Deployment Management | Release Management, Deployment Management | Service Support, ICT Infrastructure Management | |
| Service Transition | Service Asset and Configuration Management | Configuration Management | Service Support | |
| Service Transition | Service Validation and Testing | - | Service Support | |
| Service Transition | Testing Planning and Support | - | Service Support | |
| Service Operation | Access Management | - | Security Management | |
| Service Operation | Event Management | Incident Management | ICT Infrastructure Management | |
| Service Operation | Funktion: Application Management | Application Management | Application Management | |
| Service Operation | Funktion: IT Operations Management | Operations | ICT Infrastructure Management | |
| Service Operation | Funktion: Service Desk | Funktion: Service Desk | Service Support | |
| Service Operation | Funktion: Technical Management | Technical Support | ICT Infrastructure Management | |
| Service Operation | Incident Management | Incident Management | Service Support | |
| Service Operation | Problem | Problem | Service Support | |

| | | Management | Management | | |
|---|---|---|---|---|---|
| | Service Operation | Request Fulfillment | Incident Management | Service Support | |
| | Continual Service Improvement | Business Questions for CSI | - | - | |
| | Continual Service Improvement | Service Measurement | - | - | |
| | Continual Service Improvement | Return on Investment for CSI | - | - | |
| | Continual Service Improvement | Service Reporting | Teil des Service Level Management | Service Delivery | |
| | Continual Service Improvement | The 7-Step Improvement Process | - | - | |

3.g Würden Sie basierend auf Ihrem Wissen und Ihrer Erfahrung eine vollständige Einführung von ITIL Version 2 oder 3 heute gesamtheitlich angehen, welche Prozesse würden Sie einführen? Beachten Sie bitte das dafür skizzierte Szenario. Kombinieren Sie bitte die ITIL Prozesse und Funktionen sinngemäß zu Arbeitspaketen für deren Einführung.

**Szenario: Unternehmens-interne IT-Abteilung oder externer IT-Provider als Cost Center oder Profit Center mit eigenentwickelten Systemen und/oder Standardsystemen (Out-of-the-box, best-of-breed) im Betrieb.**

| ITIL framework in version 3 | Process or function in version 3 | Process or function in version 2 | ITIL framework in version 2 | Hier bitte Arbeitspaket-nummerierung eintragen |
|---|---|---|---|---|
| Service Strategy | Demand Management | Capacity Management | Service Delivery | |
| Service Strategy | Financial Management | Financial Management for IT-Services | Service Delivery | |
| Service Strategy | Service Portfolio Management | - | Business Perspective | |
| Service Strategy | Strategy Generation | - | Business Perspective | |
| Service Design | Availability Management | Availability Management | Service Delivery | |
| Service Design | Capacity Management | Capacity Management | Service Delivery | |
| Service Design | Information Security Management | Security Management | Security Management | |
| Service Design | IT Service Continuity Management | IT Service Continuity Management | Service Delivery | |
| Service Design | Service Catalogue Management | Service Level Management | Service Delivery | |
| Service Design | Service Level Management | Service Level Management | Service Delivery | |
| Service Design | Supplier Management | - | Service Delivery | |
| Service Transition | Change Management | Change Management | Service Support | |
| Service Transition | Evaluation | - | Service Support | |
| Service Transition | Knowledge Management | - | Service Support | |
| Service Transition | Release and Deployment Management | Release Management, Deployment | Service Support, ICT Infrastructure Management | |

# Appendix

| | | Management | | |
|---|---|---|---|---|
| Service Transition | Service Asset and Configuration Management | Configuration Management | Service Support | |
| Service Transition | Service Validation and Testing | - | Service Support | |
| Service Transition | Testing Planning and Support | - | Service Support | |
| Service Operation | Access Management | - | Security Management | |
| Service Operation | Event Management | Incident Management | ICT Infrastructure Management | |
| Service Operation | Funktion: Application Management | Application Management | Application Management | |
| Service Operation | Funktion: IT Operations Management | Operations | ICT Infrastructure Management | |
| Service Operation | Funktion: Service Desk | Funktion: Service Desk | Service Support | |
| Service Operation | Funktion: Technical Management | Technical Support | ICT Infrastructure Management | |
| Service Operation | Incident Management | Incident Management | Service Support | |
| Service Operation | Problem Management | Problem Management | Service Support | |
| Service Operation | Request Fulfillment | Incident Management | Service Support | |
| Continual Service Improvement | Business Questions for CSI | - | - | |
| Continual Service Improvement | Service Measurement | - | - | |
| Continual Service Improvement | Return on Investment for CSI | - | - | |
| Continual Service Improvement | Service Reporting | Teil des Service Level Management | Service Delivery | |
| Continual Service Improvement | The 7-Step Improvement Process | - | - | |

# Appendix B

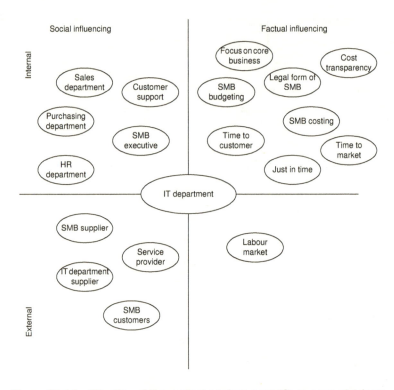

**Figure 35: Identification of the project environment (Case example) (own illustration 2009, cf. Patzak et al 2009, p.94)**

# Appendix C

| Person/ Pressure group | Attitude to IT depart- ment | Power, Influ- ence | Conflict potential | + Prospects, - Fears | Measures, strategies |
|---|---|---|---|---|---|
| SMB executive | Positive | High | Low | + More transparency of IT costs<br>+ Quicker response on change requests<br>+ Reduction of time to market<br>- Disruption in organisation<br>- Raise of IT costs | • Continuous reporting |
| Sales department | Negative | High | High | + Quicker response on change requests<br>- IT functionality is not equal to business needs<br>- Online availability of field equipment is inadequate<br>- Time to customer is too long because of weak IT services | • Involvement of sales department in organisational change project of IT department<br>• Participant in project steering committee<br>• Continuous reporting |
| ... | ... | ... | ... | ... | • ... |

**Table 19: Validation of the environment and detailed analysis (own illustration 2009, cf. Patzak et al, p. 98)**

Jochen Höfenstock                                                         130

# Appendix D

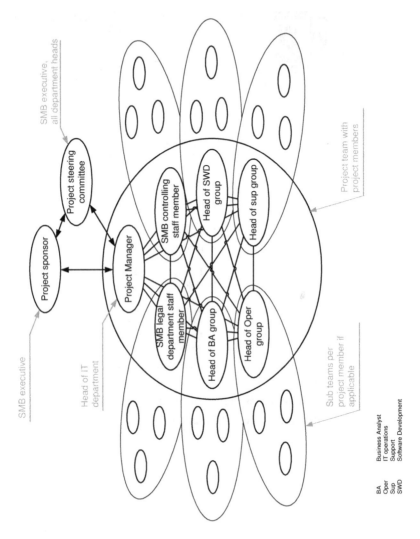

**Figure 36: ITIL implementation project organisation (Case example) (own illustration 2009, cf. Patzak et al 2009, p. 705)**

# Appendix E

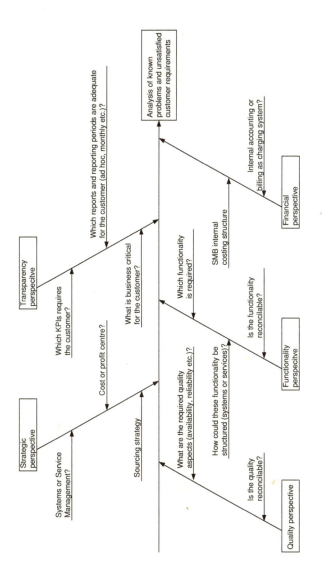

**Figure 37: Cause and effect diagram for ITIL implementation (Case example)**
**(own illustration 2009, cf. PMI 2008, p. 209f.)**

# Appendix F

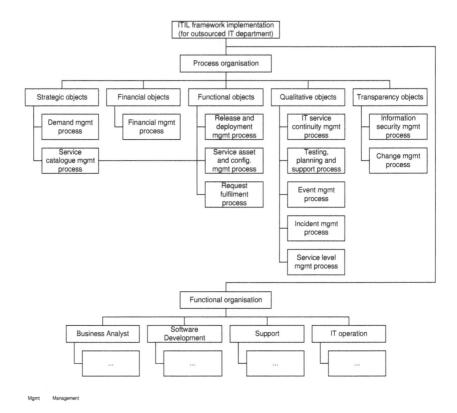

Figure 38: Object breakdown structure for ITIL implementation (Case
example) (own illustration 2009, cf. PMA 2009, p. 28)

Appendix

# Appendix G

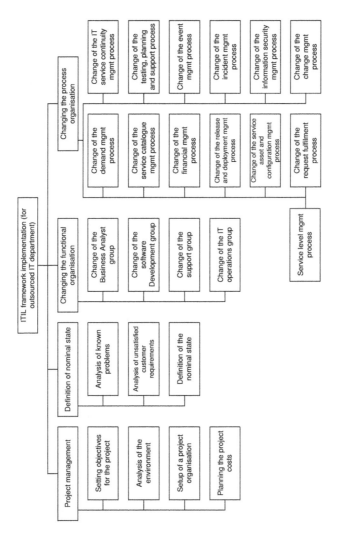

**Figure 39: Work breakdown structure for ITIL implementation (Case example) (own illustration 2009, cf. PMA 2009, p. 29)**

# Appendix H

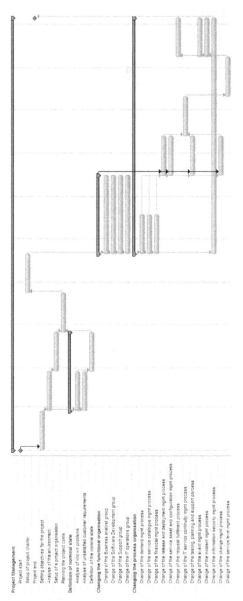

**Figure 40: Bar chart for ITIL implementation (Case example) (own illustration 2009)**

# YOUR KNOWLEDGE HAS VALUE